OVERCOME
SEXUAL URGES and ADDICTIONS

Tonyeluwa

fulfill purpose in the
name of Jesus. Amen

God bless you richly

14/oct/2022

OVERCOME
SEXUAL URGES and ADDICTIONS
Practical solutions, principles, experiences & deep spiritual mysteries

Topics Covered:
- Masturbation
- Pornography
- Fornication
- Lust
- Unwanted Sexual Arousal
- Incubus and Succubus (Spirit Spouses)
- Demonic interference
- Deliverance
- Choice, spirit, soul, and body
- What to do after breaking up

TONYCLINTON CHISOM NWEKE

XULON PRESS

Xulon Press
2301 Lucien Way #415
Maitland, FL 32751
407.339.4217
www.xulonpress.com

OVERCOME SEXUAL URGES and ADDICTIONS

Practical solutions, principles, explanations, experiences, strategies, prayer points, scriptural support, and deep spiritual mysteries.

TOPICS COVERED:

★Masturbation
★Pornography
★Fornication
★Lust
★Unwanted Sexual Arousal
★Incubus and Succubus (Spirit Spouses)
★Demonic interference
★Deliverance
★Choice, spirit, soul, and body
★What to do after breaking up

TONYCLINTON CHISOM NWEKE

CONTENT

DEDICATION

I dedicate this book to God the Father, who continuously poured out His grace and mercy as I wrote. To Jesus Christ who delivered me from the sin of masturbation, pornography, fornication, lust, and moments of extreme sexual arousal in a single day in the corner of my room. And to the Holy Spirit, who inspired me throughout the process.

ACKNOWLEDGEMENTS

I thank my father Tony U. Nweke, Mother Vivian, and siblings Collins, Chelsea, Prisca, Claire, and Kingsley for their love and support.

I acknowledge and thank my spiritual mentors Lawrence Ogechukwu, Joseph Molokwu, and Apostle Israel Egesionu for their prayers and support.

I acknowledge the ministry and teachings of Rev. Fr. Dr. Anthony Mario Ozele

FOREWORD

This book surely is an effective balm to help resolve and heal the challenges of the cancer in the church called sexual immorality and lust that have been afflicting the church of God on Earth with so many wounds and setbacks. The pages of this book contain practical experiences and recommendations that can resolve all forms of sexual immorality and lust challenges and the powers of hell promoting them to their knees. Going through this book will certainly inspire you to a higher moral and spiritual ground. God bless you as you read on in the name of Jesus Christ of Nazareth.

- Joseph JohnPaul Molokwu

For decades, the topic of sex has been silenced by society, government, and especially religious organizations. Due to cultural reasons, in some parts of the world, it was forbidden for anyone, particularly teenagers, to ask questions about sexuality. The topic was considered taboo and even married women weren't allowed to express their sexual needs to their husbands. The taboo continued till around the 18th century when the sexual revolution took place. The revolution gained momentum and it was finally taken seriously at the dawn of the 19th century. It was then the government realized sex education should be implemented in the school curriculum, even though many have disagreed and the idea only became acceptable in the 20th century. The lack of sex education led teenagers to explore the Internet and many pornographic sites, which only increased masturbation, rapes, and fornication.

We live in a world that has issues containing alarmingly high levels of sex abuse. Society and regulatory bodies are waking up a little too late to try and save the dignity of men and women, and more so, the will of God of what is good for man. God created man alone and gave him guidelines to follow when connecting with others. But man decided to sin and rebel against God, mostly when it comes to the matters of sex. It may be that man wanted to have the freedom like the animals do, to have sex with no restrictions or boundaries, and not have it imputed as a sin. And why is that so? God created man in his own image. But God is triune, meaning He represents three co-eternal persons; the Father, the Son, and the Holy Spirit John 28:19. Therefore, for man to represent God, he needs to resemble Him in body, soul, and spirit. Besides, God also promised to send the Holy Spirit and fulfill it in the book of Acts 2: 1-4.

Since God lives in man by the ways of the Holy Spirit, making him complete and fulfilled, the same way, when a man is joined in marriage he becomes one with his significant other. This is especially depicted during the intercourse when the two bodies essentially become one. So, whenever the act occurs outside of the marriage union, which was instituted by God, He is displeased. The devil always seeks for man to rebel against God and does everything in its power to lure him into pervasive, sexual acts. As we can witness today, social media, television, and even billboards are filled with seductive and pornographic pictures and materials.

Today, God gave to his servant, Tonyclinton, the opportunity to share his knowledge and experiences. With practical principles and prayer, he will reveal how one can be freed from the clutches of masturbation and fornication. It is a book recommended for anyone; parents, teachers, religious leaders, or youth. Be blessed as you read.

- Lawrence Ogechukwu

INTRODUCTION

God created sex for human beings, but who said some spirit beings do not engage in sex with humans? Some scientists classify humans as higher animals overflowing with sexual passion and desire. Is the social acceptance of this classification the reason for the animalistic behavior of some humans? Others believe that it is human nature to desire sex and so natural for unmarried persons to engage in it. Might this belief be the reason why so many people become slaves to their sexual desires?

Sex is an approved and pleasurable act that God created, but only for those married and only between a man and a woman. It yields God's blessings if done in the context of marriage, but a curse under the wrong conditions. Sexual love, or Eros, is like a fire that destroys everything it comes across. It can set ablaze and consume without pity the person who lights it. Untamed Eros becomes possessive and turns its master into a slave. It kindles ungodly sexual urges that may present themselves as raging storms or unscalable mountains.

It is fallacy to believe that sexual urges cannot be controlled or even subdued. In fact, it can be eradicated instantly. I am living proof of this claim. Since addiction to ungodly sexual urges are triggered by the influence of an evil spirit, the means of overcoming them is inspired by a different spirit. As the apostle Paul wrote: "There's more to sex than mere skin on skin. Sex is as much spiritual mystery as physical act. As written in Scripture, *'The two become one'*" (1 Corinthians 6:16 MSG). Since sex is both a physical and spiritual activity, the means of overcoming immoral sexual urges are also physical and spiritual.

This book offers solutions to a problem that has beset the human race for ages. But no one likes to discuss it because it comes with shame and stigma. The topics deal with issues that unbelievers, Christians, including Christian ministers, find challenging. The first being spiritual mysteries that reveal the interference of evil spirits in ungodly sexual engagements. You will find prayers of knowledge and deliverance for the operation of the spirit husband, or Incubus, and the spirit wife, or Succubus. Also included are practical solutions, principles, explanations, and strategies. You will find examples of biblical characters who engaged in sexual immorality. And stories of personal experience about overcoming one's addiction to masturbation, pornography, fornication (premarital sex). And even lust and moments of extreme sexual arousal.

Many engaged in sexual immorality desire deliverance from their sexual urges and addictions. And they become confused because they often return to those sexual immoral acts. Not understanding why this cycle repeats itself, they lose all hope. This book is a light in the tunnel. It provides the hope, knowledge, solution, deliverance, and guidance needed to achieve self-control. Adherence to the principles and solutions in this book will transform you and illuminate the darkness. What you will learn in this book can result in the death of ungodly sexual urges by rapid starvation and demise.

Other topics discussed in this book are the differences among spirit, soul, and body and the mechanism and pathway of their functioning and interrelation. Some other topics discussed are: how to know when a sexual urge has become an addiction; the difference between lust and love; what to do after a break-up; reasons why prayers can be left unanswered; the means through which spirit spouses gain access to a person's life; the court of heaven; things that can happen when deliverance from a spirit of perversion is lost; how to discern the spirit of perversion; the effects of the operation of spirit spouses; the essence of grace in overcoming sexual sins of the flesh; repentance and ways to live a fruitful Christian lifestyle through brokenness, daily consecration, perfect obedience, understanding the will of God, service, testing, and conscious holiness.

Since sexual purity is a matter of life and death, this book provides a means of ensuring sexual discipline together with developing a consistent life of intimacy and koinonia (communion or fellowship) with God. This is done to obtain freedom from the yoke of sexual immorality and secure God's interference in the quest for sexual purity.

This book was not accidental. It is a product of the revival that God has willed to spring forth over all nations. The aim of this book is to restore your freedom through the person of Jesus Christ and ultimately add your name in the Book of Life. On the other hand, it will contribute another foot to the offspring of the woman who will bruise the head of the serpent, and snatch souls from Satan's hands. We give glory to God because the secrets of obtaining deliverance from ungodly sexual urges, those that Satan has concealed from the Church, have now been revealed to us.

Chapter 1:

MASTURBATION

Masturbation is the ungodly stimulation of the male or female genitals through the use of hands, body parts, or external objects. Its purpose is sexual gratification that results in sexual climax. It is a common practice among youths and adults, even if rarely spoken about. Let us explore some questions and statements that might arise about such acts.

- Is masturbation a sin?
- If masturbation is a sin, where is it discussed in the Bible?
- Masturbation might be a sin for others, but not for me.
- Almost everyone masturbates.
- I was told that masturbation is a healthy practice and lowers the risk of getting a certain kind of disease.

Let us start with the faulty popular opinion, that masturbation is all right and not a sin. What is sin? Sin is the unconscious or conscious disobedience to God and a violation of His laws and principles. If sin is a violation of this, then the next question should be, does masturbation violate God's laws? If so, where is it discussed in the Bible? The word "masturbation" was coined years after the Bible was written, but the act existed long before the coinage. We must, therefore, look beyond the word and focus on the action to see whether it violates God's laws.

Through His servant Moses, God gave the Israelites commandments and laws. An issue arose but about the limitations of those who were under the law. All men who faced these limitations required a savior. As in The Book of Romans, the issue was never the law.

> *What shall we say, then? Is the law sinful? Certainly not! Nevertheless, I would not have known what sin was had it not been for the law. For I would not have known what coveting really was if the law had not said, "You shall not covet." I found that the very commandment that was intended to bring life actually brought death. Romans 7:7; 10 (NIV)*

Through this scripture we are made aware of the importance of laws and commandments. They were made for us to know what angers God and what glorifies Him. Again, the *Book of Romans* says:

> *Therefore no one will be declared righteous in God's sight by the works of the law; rather, through the law we become conscious of our sin. Romans 3:20 (NIV)*

The law reminds the people of the punishments prepared for the violators, but the law could not make a man righteous. It revealed to the people their sins but could not remove them. In the Book of Acts, we see that the law became an unbearable burden.

Now then, why do you try to test God by putting on the necks of Gentiles a yoke that neither we nor our ancestors have been able to bear? Acts 15:10 (NIV)

Human nature was the greatest limitation to the law's full expression and potential. Human beings were never created to be independent of God, but rather to be dependent on Him. It was the disobedience of Adam and Eve in the Garden of Eden that altered God's blueprint for the human race. It made the earth and the rest of creation antagonistic to man. The spirit of the Lord departed, and the limitations of the human race increased. That spirit poured out upon men on the day of Pentecost. Through this process, we can clearly see man's weakness. We see how helpless and unrighteous he would have remained had Jesus not extended His righteousness and grace. For humans to interpret and apply the law, the Holy Spirit must be present. Because the Holy Spirit led Jesus in His human nature, He was able to achieve the law's purpose. This is something Man hadn't been able to achieve. Thus, we read in the *Book of Romans*:

...that the "law" of the Spirit of life flowing through the anointing of Jesus has liberated us from the "law" of sin and death. For God achieved what the law was unable to accomplish, because the law was limited by the weakness of human nature. Romans 8:2-3 (TPT)

Although Jesus was able to accomplish the law's purpose, His coming was to release grace and mercy and let the Holy Spirit rest upon man so that we not only see our weaknesses but transcend them and attain righteousness. In addition to this, He allowed men access to a better way knowing, viewing, and interpreting the law. Now the law would no longer be consulted in a book. Men would not have to travel long distances to access the books for the laws. Rather, the law would have a permanent abode in the *thoughts and heart of men*. As the *Book of Hebrews* says:

> For here is the covenant I will one day establish with the people of Israel: I will embed my laws within their thoughts and fasten them onto their hearts. I will be their loyal God and they will be my loyal people. And the result of this will be that everyone will know me as Lord! There will be no need at all to teach their fellow-citizens or brothers by saying, 'You should know the Lord Jehovah,' since everyone will know me inwardly, from the most unlikely to the most distinguished. *Hebrew 8:10-11 (TPT)*

Thus, we can no longer claim ignorance of sin. People sin when evil enters their thoughts and heart, even if the actions do not follow. A sin no longer has to be written in a book to be acknowledged as sin. The law and commandments of God are now inscribed in our thoughts and hearts. In addition, we have received extra instruments to help us know what thoughts and actions are holy or unholy. These instruments include the voice of the Holy Spirit, the conscience, and guilty feelings. The voice of the Holy Spirit is a gift only to Christians filled with the Holy Spirit. Unbelievers can only rely on their conscience and guilt feelings, while believers are given extra assistance in the form of the Holy Spirit's voice.

There are two kinds of guilt feelings. The first is the feeling that leads to condemnation that is not from God. The second is the feeling that leads to sincere repentance. It comes through admitting, acknowledging, and repenting from all sins. This means turning away from sin to God, admitting them, verbally confessing them, forsaking and renouncing them, and then asking for mercy and forgiveness. If the process is genuine, the repentant person experiences deep remorse, and tears might likely flow. This guilty feeling comes with deep conviction from the person of the Holy Spirit, and its outcome is a daily awareness of sin, a consciousness that ensures righteous living. This is the freedom God gives His children. To support these statements, let us consider the following from 2 Corinthians:

> *Now I'm overjoyed—not because I made you sad, but because your grief led you to a deep repentance. You experienced godly sorrow, and as God intended, it brought about gain for you, not loss, so that no harm has been done by us. God designed us to feel remorse over sin in order to produce repentance that leads to victory. This leaves us with no regrets. But the sorrow of the world works death. 2 Corinthians 7:9-10 (TPT).*

Now, when a person masturbates, he or she experiences a mild or even intense feeling of guilt immediately after climax. They also experience a feeling of emptiness, especially after the initial attempt. This feeling exploits the conscience component of the soul, and so both believers and unbelievers can experience it. A believer who masturbates suddenly feels regret that outweighs the few seconds of pleasure. Shame is felt even if no other person witnessed the action.

When a masturbator ignores the warnings of his conscience or despises the voice of the Holy Spirit, he consciously or unconsciously suppresses guilt feelings. Through the constant experience of guilt, shame, and fear, the masturbator is aware of his sin, but tries to justify it by suppressing the convicting voice of the Holy Spirit.

Many people feel guilt, fear, and shame whenever they fall short of God's standards. Adam and Eve, the first human beings, felt the same when they disobeyed God by eating the forbidden fruit. It is in man's blueprint to feel this way whenever they violate a law of God.

Masturbation requires the help of lust and sometimes pornography. Masturbation is a sin against God because it involves lust which is itself a sin. As earlier stated, an overt act is not necessary for it to be present. Instead, sin starts in the thoughts and heart, and once in the heart, it is a sin. As Jesus said in the *Book of Matthew:*

> But I tell you that anyone who looks at a woman
> lustfully has already committed adultery with her
> in his heart. Matthew 5:28 (NIV)

It follows that merely lusting during masturbation makes that act a sin according to the standards of Jesus. Some people hold an odd belief that masturbation is a sin for others when they practice it, but not for themselves. That belief is false and based on a fallacy. Once the feeling of guilt, fear, or shame takes hold, that is enough to indicate that it violates God's principles. The fact that many people practice it, including false teachers, does not make it righteous. From history, we learned that most people do not align their will with God's will. Their opinions about God's laws do not change them; if the majority sins, He does not spare His wrath. The seventh chapter of the *Book of Genesis* gives an example of God's decision to punish the human race with a flood for their wicked acts. Only eight people were saved. Jesus, who is the judge, also stated in the *Book of Matthew*: "Enter by the narrow gate; for wide is the gate and broad is the way that leads to destruction, and there are many who go in by it. Because narrow is the gate and difficult is the way which leads to life, and there are few who find it" (Matthew 7:13-14). It is therefore obvious that God does not bend His rules for anyone. No matter the reason man gives, what He considers sin will not change.

Lastly, some scientific researchers promote masturbation as a "healthy practice that lowers the risk of getting a certain kind of disease." As believers of the gospel, we are to be observant and discerning. Our wisdom is superior to the world's wisdom because we are gifted with the wisdom of the Holy Spirit. Satan is a strategist who uses lucrative and enticing ways to deceive people. He may use the same strategies but, unknown to many people, his goal is to kill, steal, and destroy (John 10:10). When he decides to deceive a nation, he targets the administrators, the leaders of religious, scientific, and governmental institutions. With craft and cunningness, he gets the attention and cooperation of people. Satan does this even in scientific institutions, as he did when he deceived Adam and Eve in the Garden of Eden. He told Eve that if she were to eat from the tree, her eyes will open, and she will know good and evil. These statements were correct, but then Satan deceitfully added that she and Adam would not die. Hidden in his words was his true intention; to make them anger God and lose their koinonia (communion and fellowship) with Him. Adam and Eve fell for Satan's trick.

Before accepting a research outcome, you should use your spiritual senses to screen the procedures and findings. First, identify the goal and consider its possible effects on the nation, the body of the Christ (Church), and your eternal life. Second, identify the hidden agenda and connect it to your faith in Jesus Christ. I have advised this because we are in the last days and every evil thing is possible. Finally, ask questions. If you do not find genuine, spirit-filled answers, do not believe or practice what you have heard. Here are some questions:

- Are there no other ways to prevent the risk of getting such a disease?
- Why is masturbation the suggested method?
- Will my masturbating upset God?
- Is my physical well-being more important than my eternal life?
- How ought I choose between pleasure and God?
- Would Satan benefit from my actions?
- Why must I sin to avoid a disease I may never get?
- Is the wisdom of a scientist superior to God's?
- Can God save and heal me from any disease?

After asking these questions, if you are sincere, you can arrive at only one conclusion: masturbation is *not* necessary. It has no benefit for a Christian, eternal or temporal. It upsets God and can damn your soul to hell.

*The thief comes only to steal and kill and destroy;
I have come that they may have life and have it to
the full. John 10:10 (NIV)*

Voice of the Holy Spirit, the
conscience, and guilty feelings

DEMONIC INTERFERENCE DURING
THE ACT OF MASTURBATION

The concept of demonic interference during masturbation is
familiar to some. The first question one might ask is, how
and why would a demon assist a person in masturbation?
Let me begin by bringing to your awareness the existence
of two realms, that of the spirit and the physical. The spirit
realm cannot be seen with the human eye unless God permits it, while the physical realm is the realm we perceive with
our senses. When we pray to God, our mouths express the
intention of our heart. Those prayers then ascend like incense
to God in the spirit realm. He either accepts or rejects them.
The believer's goal is to connect to the spirit realm daily, consciously or unconsciously. Likewise, it is the goal of spirit
beings to connect with humans in the physical realm.

In fact, most events that occur in the physical realm are
planned and known in the spirit realm. They only manifest
in the physical realm at a later time. Consider the event
reported in the *Book of 1 Kings*, Chapter 22. Israel's King

Ahab was about to go to war. He summoned 400 prophets and asked them if he should go into battle. They all told him to proceed with the war and added that the Lord will give him victory. Another monarch, Jehoshaphat, king of Judah, was with Israel's King Ahab that day. Jehoshaphat asked if there was another prophet he could consult. Ahab replied: "there is still one prophet through whom we can inquire of the Lord, but I hate him because he never prophesies anything good about me, but always bad. He is Micaiah son of Imlah" 1 Kings 22:8 (NIV). The King then asked for Prophet Micaiah to be summoned. The messengers who had gone to summon Micaiah said to him, "Look, the other prophets without exception are predicting success for the king. Let your word agree with theirs and speak favorably" 1 Kings 22:13(NIV). Prophet Micaiah arrived before the King and was questioned if he could go on with the war against Ramoth Gilead. At first Micaiah responded by saying, "Attack and be victorious, for the Lord will give it into the king's hand" 1 Kings 22:15 (NIV). But the king said to him, "How many times must I make you swear to tell me nothing but the truth in the name of the Lord?" 1 Kings 22:16 (NIV) Prophet Micaiah replied: "In a vision I saw Israelite soldiers walking around in the hills like sheep without a shepherd to guide them. The LORD said, "This army has no leader. They should go home and not fight" 1 Kings 22:17 (CEV). Micaiah continued, "Listen to this! I also saw the Lord seated on his throne with every creature in heaven gathered around him. The Lord asked, "Who can trick Ahab and make him go to Ramoth where he will be killed?" They talked about it for a while, then finally a spirit came forward and said to the Lord, "I can trick Ahab." "How?" the Lord asked. "I'll make Ahab's prophets lie to him." "Good!" the Lord replied. "Now go and do it" 1 Kings 22:19-22 (CEV).

Upon hearing this Ahab asked his official to lock up Micaiah. He chose to believe the 400 prophets, fought and died in that battle.

From this true biblical story, we understand that the spirit realm influences outcomes in the physical realm. Many occurrences that we tag as random or coincidental are actually planned and finalized by spirit beings. Every law of God that is violated in the physical realm is noted in the spirit realm and has consequences. The spirit realm is a kingdom and operates like one. When a human being decides to make God his master, the Holy Spirit fills him, and the evil spirits leave him. But when a human being rebels against God, or sins against Him directly or indirectly, the Holy Spirit departs and an evil spirit possesses him or her. The life of a human being permits no vacuum. Therefore, a spirit must always have some expression in our lives, whether for good or bad, depending on the spirit.

Since God considers masturbation a sin against Him, His spirit departs from the presence of masturbators. An evil spirit, in this case "an unclean spirit," takes control of the masturbator. This is done with or without that person's knowledge or permission. Unclean spirits possess and manipulate masturbators as they wish. They can sense when and where the act takes place and find their way there. As a person masturbates, these spirits watch and partake in the act. Instilling unclean thoughts and contaminating the heart of such a person. The sinner cannot see these spirits with his or her physical eyes unless God permits it.

Sometimes unclean spirits work alongside spirit spouses. A male spirit spouse is known as incubus; a female spirit spouse, succubus. Such spirits can appear in the dreams of masturbators and engage in sexual intercourse with the masturbator. But often they disguise their identity by using the faces of people the sinner knows. These can be friends, celebrities, or past and present partners in sexual immorality. The unclean spirits can bear children for their victims, keeping them in the spirit realm. There have been cases where the spirits appear in the physical to their victim using these spirit children. When they appear, they may commit sexual assault on their victims or harm them in other ways.

This unclean spirit's technique of disclosing, masquerading, or using a different identity in dreams keeps its victims ignorant of that spirit's presence. Some prefer to keep their victims unaware so that their control over their lives is not ended through repentance, prayers, fasting, or deliverance. In other victims, these spirits engage in a higher level of identity concealment. They do not appear in their victims' dreams. By doing this, the unclean spirits keep their victims unaware of their presence as they continue to manipulate their victim's times, seasons, and destinies.

> When a human being decides to make God his master, the Holy Spirit, that is, the spirit of God which is also "Light," fills him, and the evil spirits are forced to depart.

ADDICTION TO MASTURBATION

Masturbation is one of the most addictive acts a person can engage in. Many addicts try to disengage from the act, but in vain. The more they try to stop, the more they engage in it. That's because masturbation is aided by an unclean spirit.

When people initially engage in the practice of masturbation, they possess some level of self-control. After some time, they lose that self-control. As they derive pleasure from the act, they reject the voice of the Holy Spirit or the warnings of their conscience. This rejection causes an unclean spirit to find its way into their lives. At that point, masturbation becomes an addiction.

A sign of the presence of such spirit is the loss of self-control. For instance, if masturbators attempt to limit their engagement in masturbation to twice a month, once the unclean spirit is involved, they will violate that limit and find themselves masturbating once a week and then many times a week. They often rely on masturbation as a stress-reliever, eventually becoming a slave to their flesh.

The presence of such an unclean spirit causes a loss of self-will in several areas of their life, causing an inability to control sexual urges. Marriage is never a solution for masturbation, especially when an unclean spirit is involved. It will certainly be carried over to marriage if not dealt with before. In fact, an unclean spirit is excited when the addiction is carried over to marriage and uses it as an opportunity to destroy marriages. The good news is that there is a cure for addictive masturbation, and we will explore the solutions.

MY STORY

I was born in Nigeria and received my secondary school education there. One day at boarding school, I walked into the room of some fellow borders. I found what I saw very strange, shocking, and amusing at the same time. They were masturbating on their beds. I could not fathom the meaning of what they were doing or why they were doing it. I was confused, because I had never before seen people engaging in such an act. I stood at the entrance of the room and stared at them. I saw the amusement and excitement they derived from what they were doing. I had so many questions. Smiling at me, they invited me in, but that only threw me into a deeper state of confusion. I decided to do what I saw them doing so I could experience the same feeling. I soon realized I was not deriving the same pleasure. I remained perplexed and confused. All of a sudden, a thought flashed through my mind, the thought of a dream I once had. In it I engaged in sexual immorality. Remembering this dream was an opportunity for me to dwell on an ungodly dream. As soon as this happened, I was able to achieve maximal sexual satisfaction.

My excitement lasted a while but soon diminished and ended with an immense feeling of guilt. I began to engage in this act whenever I was idle. It became an addiction. I perfected this act, and although I would feel some guilt on occasion, I tried to subdue it.

Before becoming a boarding student, I was a member of a powerful prayer unit in the Catholic Church known as the Catholic Charismatic Renewal of Nigeria. It was through one of its programs called "Life in the Spirit Seminar" at Catholic

Church of the Holy Spirit Omole Lagos that I gave my life to Christ and was Spirit filled at the age of nine. I became a member of the healing ministry and began to grow in Christ. I was a zealous member and became a lover of God. But my zeal and prayer fire decreased as the practice of masturbation took hold of my life.

For my undergraduate studies, I emigrated from Nigeria to Canada. The addiction to masturbate intensified in Canada. I became prayerless, less interested in the things of God. When I lived in a student residence, there was a fellow resident whose room was directly above mine. He would often bring his girlfriend over, and the noise they made during sexual intercourse kept me awake. I would hear things falling to the floor, panting, heavy breathing, and loud moaning. I was relieved when I no longer heard the sound, but the relief wouldn't last, for they would shortly resume intercourse. I would get frustrated and thoughts to masturbate filled my mind.

All these embarrassed me and affected my relationship with God. Since I was raised a Catholic, I would normally confess my sins to God through a priest. At some point I stopped going to confession. I was tired of confessing the same sins and was embarrassed to name them to the priest. I was also tired of confessing and returning to the sins I had just confessed. I felt I was cheating God and needed to stop deceiving myself. Eventually I stopped serving at Sunday Mass (I was an altar server) and even stopped attending. Sometimes I prayed asking God to overcome this habit. On the other hand, I was pleased with the gratification I derived from masturbation. Because my prayers were filled with unbelief, I never got the help I then needed.

My story continues in the next chapter but let me make a few observations. Notice how my boarding schoolmates made the act look cool when I caught them in the act and how, smiling, they invited me to join them; how Satan strategically planted a dream of sexual immorality some time before I was introduced to the act; how I had to dwell on lustful thoughts before I could derive satisfaction from masturbating; how I was filled with guilt after the act and tried suppressing it over the years; how my awareness of someone's else's sexual inter-course was the occasion of my masturbation; how I stopped going to confession, serving at Mass, stopped attending masses for years, and progressively got less interested in the things of God; how masturbation became an addiction. Finally, notice how in my unbelief I prayed for help, but was still interested in the act.

PRACTICAL SOLUTIONS FOR MASTURBATION

1. Ultimate and Instant Deliverance from Masturbation

Although masturbation can be addictive, it is different from other kinds of addiction. There are ways to control it, but once an unclean spirit is involved, the preferred solution is deliverance. Deliverance can only be received through Jesus Christ. He determines the process and duration of the deliver-ance He alone gives, but deliverance from the unclean spirit facilitating the masturbation can occur in a split second.

To receive this deliverance, you must resolve never to mastur-bate again. You must see Jesus as your only source of help and resolve to keep praying until you are delivered. Jesus hears all our thoughts and sees all our actions. He is a jealous God Who you can never share. If you have plans to return to your previous sinful practice, doubt His ability to help you, or decide to consult other gods and spiritual mediums, you will not receive the deliverance you desire. Deliverance is a two-way street: you decide, pray, and take physical measures, while Jesus engages in the spiritual aspect. Every spiritual battle has already been won through the death and triumphant resurrection of Jesus Christ. He paid the price and took up your sins and burdens. Therefore, all you need to do is to align yourself with and enter into the merits of His death and resurrection. You must decide to be disgusted and irritated by masturbation. Visualize it as coming from an unclean spirit and hate it for trying to destroy you.

Jesus only intervenes when you have made up your mind against masturbation, repented and hated the act, resolving not to return to it, and then trusting in His saving power. You must ask for God's mercy and grace. His mercy moves Him to cleanse you of all your sins and help you. You must realize that *only* He has the power to save and deliver you from the unclean spirit of masturbation. Comprehending this reality will make you approach Him with sincerity, seriousness, and all your heart. God does not answer the prayers of people who do not seek Him with all their heart. As Jeremiah prophesied: *"You will seek me and find me when you seek me with all your heart." Jeremiah 29:13 (NIV)*

Therefore, the intensity of your prayer and the decision you make determine the actions that Jesus will take.

Whenever we pray and seek help, Jesus measures our seriousness. He stands at the door of your heart saying:

> *Come to me, all you who are weary and burdened, and I will give you rest. Take my yoke upon you and learn from me, for I am gentle and humble in heart, and you will find rest for your souls. For my yoke is easy and my burden is light. Matthew 11:28-30 (NIV)*

It is because of your situation that He died on the cross. He came so that His blood will pay the price of your deliverance. He came so that unclean spirits would have no hold over you again, as Isaiah prophesied: *"But he was pierced for our transgressions; he was crushed for our iniquities; upon him was the chastisement that brought us peace, and with his wounds we are healed." (Isaiah 53:5 ESV)*

Jesus is pleased when you have peace, and He is eager to help you. He is waiting for you to decide to seek Him for help with *all of your heart,* the moment you decide to allow Him into your life to help you. He is waiting for you to decide you no longer want to return to your past ways. Once He finds you in this state, He chases the unclean spirit out of your life and immediately sets you free.

The time for deliverance is *now.* To show your readiness for it, you can do the following:

1. Follow the instructions in the section of this book entitled *Four Steps to Receiving Salvation,* starting with repentance towards God, then faith in Jesus, water

baptism, and Holy Spirit baptism. Make sure to say the salvation prayer in that section.

2. Believe that *only* Jesus can save you and seek Him with all of your heart.
3. Throw away all sexually immoral devices you used while masturbating. Delete all sexually immoral pictures on your devices, including those of your ex-boyfriends, ex-girlfriends, celebrities, and strangers.
4. Resolve never to return to your old ways again
5. Say the Prayer of Dedication (Appendix 1).
6. Say the Prayer of Deliverance from Masturbation (Appendix 1).

Now that you have followed these instructions, I pray that the hand of the Lord will be stretched forth upon you and that you receive deliverance from every unclean spirit instigating and encouraging your masturbation, in the name of Jesus Christ, Amen.

Giving Jesus authority over your life allows His Spirit to fill you, and so your self-control or self-will is restored. Once you restore self-control, it is again within your power to align either with the will of God or the will of Satan and his demons. Demons see humans they once possessed as their property. They themselves do not have a body through which to find expression; they get excited when they find a person that they can possess and manipulate. They become enraged when evicted from a human body and desire to return to it. As Jesus declared:

> *When a demon is cast out of a person, it goes to wander in the waterless realm, searching for rest.*

But finding no place to rest it says, 'I will go back to the body of the one I left.' When it returns, it finds the person like a house that has been swept clean and made tidy but is empty. Then it goes and enlists seven demons more evil than itself, and they all enter and possess the person, leaving that one with a much worse fate than before. Luke 11:24-26 (TPT)

These demons return to see if this person is tidy and empty, and if he or she is, they invite seven spirits, even more evil, to help it keep its stronghold. You can read more about some of these demons that can return in Chapter 7: Deliverance, in the subsection "What Happens When Deliverance from the Spirit of Perversion is Lost?"

A question that might arise from Luke 11:24-26 is, what does it mean for a person to be made tidy but empty? It means several things:

It means the person who had just received deliverance has gone back to their sins and past ways. It means they are not making enough effort to sustain an adequate prayer life and power-filled Christian lifestyle. It also means they are not bearing fruit for God. And also means that they do not effectively communicate with and hear back from God. If persons delivered are not making the necessary effort, they can lose their deliverance; their case can become worse than before. The other solutions and principles explained below will help to sustain deliverance from an unclean spirit that facilitates masturbation.

2. The Principle of Discarding Sexual Object, Tools, and Toys

The principle of discarding sexual objects is a principle that attracts God's intervention. This is because it shows God your readiness and willingness to quit masturbating. One way to discern the heart of God is to study examples of His dealing with His people, especially the Israelites as recorded in Scripture. It pleases God when we get rid of items that caused us to rebel and sin against Him. It is recorded in the *Book of Exodus* that when Moses went to commune with God, the Israelites molded a golden calf with their jewelry and made it their god. This act was disrespectful to the Almighty God who had brought them out of Egypt and protected as they journeyed. God rebuked them and refused to go with them in their journey. He asked that they first take off their jewelry before He decided what to do with them, which they did, as recorded in the *Book of Exodus*:

> For the Lord had commanded Moses to tell them,
> "You are a stubborn people. If I were to go with
> you even for a moment, I would completely destroy
> you. Now take off your jewelry, and I will decide
> what to do with you." So after they left Mount
> Sinai, the people of Israel no longer wore jewelry.
> Exodus 33:5-6 (GNT)

Along with their repentance, taking off the jewelry they used to dishonor God was important to Him. The same goes for those who seek God's mercy and deliverance from the addiction of masturbation. You must first discard any and every object, tool, and toy that you used in the practice before God decides to intervene. Keeping them will increase the desire to return to the same act and give Satan an opportunity to tempt you. These sexual objects will also stimulate ungodly sexual desires since they are already associated with the practice of masturbation. A list of such sexual objects includes toys, lubricants, condoms, contraceptives, sex ramps (if unmarried), vibrators, and all other sexual items that no unmarried person should possess.

To store such items in your garage, attic, or warehouse is not the same as discarding them. The goal is to reject what they represent and show God your repentance and readiness to receive His help. There is a proper way to discard such items: put them in the garbage or waste bin and, if it's possible to do, burn them. But before getting rid of them, pray to dissociate yourselves from the spirits. You may use the prayer provided in Appendix 1 entitled "Prayer before Discarding Sexual Objects Used for Masturbation." After praying, sprinkle the oil and water on the items. If an ordained minister has not blessed them, you can do it yourself by praying. These prayers are in Appendix 2 entitled "Prayer to Bless the Oil and Water." After you sprinkle blessed oil and water on the items, throw them in the garbage or burn them. Praise the name of Jesus as you do so.

3. Fasting

Fasting is a productive way to sustain deliverance from an unclean spirit that facilitates masturbation. It subdues the flesh and elevates a human being's spiritual component. It increases the urge to pray and replaces the urge to masturbate. It deepens intimacy with God and increases sensitivity to spiritual things. And, it sharpens the spiritual senses, opening the spiritual eyes and ears. Fasting sets the oppressed free and breaks their yoke as Isaiah prophesied: *"Is this not the fast which I choose, to loosen the bonds of wickedness, to undo the bands of the yoke, And, to let the oppressed go free and break every yoke?" Isaiah. 58:6 (NASB)*

A fast's duration will vary according to your spiritual maturity, capacity, and need. There are a variety of durations: 6:00 a.m.-12:00 p.m., 6:00 a.m.-3:00 p.m., 6:00 p.m.-6:00 a.m., one day of dry fasting (no food for twenty-four hours), three days of dry fasting, seven days of dry fasting, forty days and forty nights fasting, and fruit and water fasting. It is good spiritual practice to increase the duration and timing of your fast as the Holy Spirit leads.

A common mistake among fasters is to stay righteous during the fast, but return to their ungodly ways. God detests such hypocrisy and will not accept such fasts. You must stay righteous all the days of your life because your Father in heaven is righteous. There are other instructions you must obey as you fast:

> *When you fast, don't look like those who pretend to be spiritual. They want everyone to know they're fasting, so they appear in public looking miserable, gloomy, and disheveled. Believe me, they've already received their reward in full. When you fast, don't let it be obvious, but instead, wash your face and groom yourself and realize that your Father in the secret place is the one who is watching all that you do in secret and will continue to reward you openly. Matthew 6: 16-18 (TPT)*

Since the ability to fast and the spiritual energy needed for it are within the Holy Spirit's power to give, you must ask Him for help. He is the only one that makes a fast possible when it seems impossible. As you fast, you will grow spiritually and reinforce your territory against the attacks of unclean spirits.

4. <u>Prayer</u>

Prayer is another form of sustaining deliverance from masturbation. It is a form of communication and koinonia (communion and fellowship) with God. As you pray, you present your needs and heart desires, but you also long to hear His voice. While praying, it is common to receive instructions from God. So, you must sharpen your spiritual senses. Prayer must be a lifestyle, not something done only when a need arises.

Prayers ascend to God like incense and can be either accepted or rejected. Here are some reasons why they could be turned away:

- Unconfessed sin: Unconfessed sins are a great hindrance to prayer. It is a reason Satan provides when he accuses people before God. Unconfessed sins separate people from God and prevents God from hearing prayers, therefore leaving them unanswered: *"But your iniquities have made a separation between you and your God, and your sins have hidden His face from you so that He does not hear." Isaiah 59:2 (ESV)*

- Doubtful prayers: Prayers said with doubts and unbelief do not please God. They prevent the angels of God from carrying out their assignments of helping us. Therefore, when you ask, you must believe and not doubt, because the one who doubts is like a wave of the sea, blown and tossed by the wind as the Apostle James wrote. When you pray you must believe that everything is possible for God to do, including delivering you from the powers and oppression of Satan: *"But when you ask, you must believe and not doubt, because the one who doubts is like a wave of the sea, blown and tossed by the wind." James 1:6 (NIV)*

- Pride: Pride upsets God and hinders the answering of prayers. It displays a person's level of immaturity and truncates spiritual progress. People who are proud believe they are self-sufficient. They attribute the end of their masturbation addiction to their efforts. "Pride brings a person low, but he who is lowly in spirit will obtain honor" Proverbs 29:23 (ESV). Being conscious of the reasons why prayers can be left unanswered will guide you on how to pray. As a result, you maintain deliverance from the powers of the unclean spirit of masturbation.

5. <u>Speaking in Tongues</u>

Speaking in tongues is speaking in a language unknown to the speaker as led by the Holy Spirit. It is also a language of angels, which human beings can speak and understand through the inspiration of the Holy Spirit. The effects of speaking in tongues are many and powerful. It is a powerful means to suppress thoughts and the urge to masturbate. It replaces them with godly and holy thoughts. Speaking in tongues is also a means through which the Holy Spirit inserts into our spirit the prayers we need to pray: *"In the same way, the Spirit helps us in our weakness. We do not know what we ought to pray for, but the Spirit himself intercedes for us through wordless groans." Romans 8:26 (NIV)*

The power of the Holy Spirit fills every spoken tongue. Tongues confuse Satan and his demons and throw them into a state of confusion. Spoken tongues also have a great effect on those who speak them. They increase the speakers' inner spirit fire and alter their environment. They also chase unclean spirits that facilitate masturbation from their vicinity.

6. The Principle of Association with Friends and Roommates

The friends with whom a person surrounds himself or her-self influence that person. The Principle of Association with Friends and Roommates subdues the urge to masturbate. As mentioned earlier, I was living in a boarding house when I learned about the act of masturbation through residents. I knew from the outset that they were not the right people for me to associate with because of their ungodly behavior, but I refused to adhere to that inner voice of the Holy Spirit. That refusal exposed me to Satan's trap.

Those you associate with have the potential to transfer their characteristics and behavior to you. So, be intentional about and conscious of the friends you have. By associating with Jesus, His apostles adopted His behavior and style of talking. When Jesus was arrested, bystanders accused the Apostle Peter of being a follower of Jesus. This was true, but Peter denied it. The bystanders insisted, however, and their evi-dence was that Peter spoke like Jesus. We may surmise that

Peter's motive was not to reflect Jesus' way of speaking, but to avoid arrest. Unknown to Peter, he had adopted Jesus' characteristics through his association with Him: *"A little later the bystanders came up and said to Peter, 'Surely you too are one of them; for even the way you talk gives you away.'"* Matthew 26:73 (NASB)

Therefore, a person who associates with light becomes light, and a person who associates with darkness becomes darkness. A person who keeps friends that masturbate with no intention of preaching the gospel of Jesus Christ to them will likely become like them. You must select the kind of friends you want to keep, utilizing the gift of discernment from the Holy Spirit. Shun sexually immoral people, and if you preach the gospel to them, do so wisely. Be guided by the wisdom of God, because the children of the world are intentional about making you like them. Satan provides them with strategies to carry out their assignments with or without their awareness. You may be free from the power of masturbation, but that does not mean that Satan has abandoned your case. He is working to get you back under the yoke of masturbation, especially through your close circle and friends: *"And the lord commended the unjust steward, because he had done wisely: for the children of this world are in their generation wiser than the children of light"* Luke 16:8 (KJV).

So, keep your spiritual senses in tune and alert. Guard your heart and involve God in every decision you make, including the kinds of friends you keep. Associate yourself with spirit-filled Christian brethren and heed the words of Apostle Paul: *"Be ye not unequally yoked together with unbelievers: for what fellowship hath righteousness with unrighteousness?*

and what communion hath light with darkness?" 2 Corinthians 6:14 (KJV).

In addition to the kind of friends you associate with, you must also be conscious of the kind of house you visit and live in. Avoid houses whose occupants continually engage in sexually immoral activities. The moaning they make when they fornicate is a means through which Satan tempts people to masturbate. Also avoid partaking in or listening to conversations that do not glorify God.

> A person who associates with light at some point becomes light, and a person who associates with darkness will at some point become darkness.

7. Avoid Pornography and Delete It from Your Electronic Devices

The eye is the gateway to the soul. Whatever you see has the power to influence you. Viewing pornographic content is one of the easiest means through which the urge of masturbation arises and unclean spirits are invited into a person's life. The presence of these unclean spirits is responsible for the sudden pressure that pushes one to masturbate, engage in sexual immorality, or imitate pornographic content. Pornography charges an atmosphere, causing sudden arousal in the viewer. Since it is pleasurable, it can be retained in the viewer's mind and resurface even days later. To satisfy the resulting urge, one option is to masturbate. To avoid this urge, a person must avoid pornography in all its forms. Go beyond that by deleting from your electronic devices any pictures and videos of anyone in a sexually immoral pose or activity, including those of former girlfriends and boyfriends, sexually immoral admirers, colleagues, strangers, and celebrities.

Chapter 2:

PORNOGRAPHY

Pornography (or "porn") is video, audio, and printed materials that stimulate ungodly sexual arousal. The consumption of pornography is abnormal by God's standards, but it is quickly becoming the statistical norm for adults, teenagers, and even children. It has become one of the greatest tools used by Satan and his agents to poison minds. Pornography invites ideas of unnatural sexual engagement in the lives of its viewers. This results in confusion. Pornographers intend to make abnormal behavior appear normal. Their motivation is to make viewers practice what they watch, thereby receiving the curses God has assigned to the commission of such acts.

The viewer of pornography is never alone. There is always an evil spirit also watching it, and it gets excited when people imitate the immoral behavior. Pornography instills in its viewers an abnormal urge to engage in immoral sexual relationships with multiple people until they find someone who can replicate the behavior they see in the pornography. When the viewer cannot find such a person, they explore other ungodly means of deriving sexual pleasure, such as rape, pedophilia, bestiality, and the use of sex toys.

The eye is a pathway to the human soul, and sometimes the brain permanently stores what the eye sees. As psalmist says: *"Turn my eyes from looking at worthless things; and give me life in your ways." Psalm 119:37 (ESV)* Viewing pornography tempts many to engage in sexual immorality. Satan is strategic about how he tempts people into sin. Most frequently he tempts them using things they might desire. In the *Book of Matthew*, we learn that after Jesus had concluded his fast of forty days and forty nights, Satan knew Jesus was hungry and decided to tempt him with food: "If you are the Son of God, tell these stones to become bread (Matthew 4:1-14). To this day, Satan continues to use this strategy to provoke humans to sin.

> *Then Jesus was led by the Spirit into the wilderness to be tempted by the devil. After fasting forty days and forty nights, he was hungry. The tempter came to him and said, "If you are the Son of God, tell these stones to become bread." Jesus answered, "It is written: 'Man shall not live on bread alone, but on every word that comes from the mouth of God.'" Matthew 4: 1-4 (NIV)*

The lust and unnatural craving in the human heart leads people to consume pornography, which gives Satan the opportunity to tempt them with sexual immorality, which sin leads to death and eternal damnation. As we read in the *Book of James*:

> *But each person is tempted when he is lured and enticed by his own desire. Then desire when it has*

conceived gives birth to sin, and sin when it is fully grown brings forth death. James 1:14-15 (ESV)

Again, the eye is a gateway to the human soul, and its misuse attracts evil consequences. Here's an example from the *Book of 2 Samuel*:

Then it happened in the spring, at the time when the kings go out to battle, that David sent Joab and his servants with him, and all [the fighting men of] Israel, and they destroyed the Ammonites and besieged Rabbah. But David remained in Jerusalem. One evening David got up from his couch and was walking on the [flat] roof of the king's palace, and from there he saw a woman bathing; and she was very beautiful in appearance. David sent word and inquired about the woman. Someone said, "Is this not Bathsheba, the daughter of Eliam, the wife of Uriah the Hittite?" David sent messengers and took her. When she came to him, he lay with her. And when she was purified from her uncleanness, she returned to her house. The woman conceived; and she sent word and told David, "I am pregnant." Then David sent word to Joab, saying, "Send me Uriah the Hittite." So Joab sent Uriah to David. When Uriah came to him, David asked him how Joab was, how the people were doing, and how the war was progressing. Then David said to Uriah, "Go down to your house, and wash your feet (spend time at home)." Uriah left the king's palace, and a gift from the king was sent out after him. But Uriah slept at the entrance of the king's palace with all the servants of his lord, and did not go down to his house. When they told David, "Uriah did not go down to his house," David said to Uriah, "Have you not [just] come from a [long] journey? Why did you not go to your house?" Uriah said to David, "The ark and Israel and Judah are staying in huts (temporary shelters), and my lord Joab and the servants of my lord are camping in the open field. Should I go to my house to eat and drink and lie with my wife? By your life and the life of your soul, I will not do this thing." Then David said to Uriah, "Stay here today as well, and tomorrow I will let you leave." So Uriah remained in Jerusalem that day and the next. Now David called him [to dinner], and he ate and drank with him, so that he made Uriah drunk; in the evening he went out to lie on his bed with the servants of his lord, and [still] did not go down to his house. In the morning David wrote a letter to Joab and sent it with Uriah. He wrote in the letter, "Put Uriah in the front line of the heaviest fighting and leave him, so that he may be struck down and die." So it happened that as Joab was besieging the city, he assigned Uriah to the place where he knew the [enemy's] valiant men were positioned. And the men of the city came out and fought against Joab, and some of the people among the servants of David fell; Uriah the Hittite also died. 2 Samul 11: 1-17 (AMP Bible)

This biblical story is a good description of the effect of pornography. We can observe how David went from watching a lady bathe, to committing adultery with her, to conspiring to hide his sin, and finally to murder. These events happened because King David lacked self-control when he saw. King David had a choice, and so do consumers of pornography. After that experience, he could have decided to avoid the roof of the king's palace at certain times of the day or resist the ungodly thoughts that flooded his mind after seeing Bathsheba naked, or even confess his sins to God and ask for a way out. Instead, he chose to cover one sin by committing another. He was unaware that the great monarch of heaven had seen his evil deed. Today, we do not need to walk on the roof of our house to see naked women. They are on our streets, buses, trains, motels, hotels, television, social media, magazines, and many other places. Even though we do not intentionally look for them, we must still be conscious of the effect they have on us. God has given us the power to overcome all temptations, and if anyone fails under this pressure, it means their strength was too small. *"If you fail under pressure, your strength is too small." Proverbs 24:10 (NLT)*

MY PORNOGRAPHY ADDICTION

As I mentioned earlier, lust facilitated the way I derived sexual gratification from masturbation. Eventually, however, lusting during masturbation did not generate enough sexual pleasure, so I added the viewing of pornography. This became easier after I moved from Nigeria to Canada. In Nigeria, the price of a data bundle was prohibitively expensive for me, a secondary school student, and thus an obstacle to viewing pornography. Things were different in Canada: it was much easier to find pornography. I was a free man, that is, without direct supervision and control by parents or anyone else.

I knew where to find pornographic sites how I could access kind of pornography I wanted. I explored as much as I wanted, surrounded by friends equally interested. I saw how much people glorified it and how many of them engaged in it.

In school I had a Muslim friend who was also yoked with the burden of masturbation and pornography. He saw it as a form of pleasure and would often spend hours with both. My hope in being delivered from this yoke decreased every time I saw him observe the fast of the thirty days of Ramadan. I felt this way because he would return to pornography and masturbation a few days or weeks later. It happened year after year, and we would sometimes laugh about it. I gave up on the idea of praying to Jesus for help.

Notice how lust was not enough for me to attain sexual gratification from masturbation, so I came to depend on viewing pornography for extra stimulation; how moving to Canada gave me more opportunities to explore pornography, to the point where I became addicted; how my friends experienced the same lust but, instead of resisting it, glorified it; how seeing my Muslim friend masturbate and consume pornography shortly after the Ramadan fast all worked against my faith in the power of prayer and my hope for deliverance.

PRACTICAL REMEDIES FOR PORNOGRAPHY ADDICTION

1. The Principle of Exchanging Appetites

The Principle of Exchanging Appetites involves substituting a bad appetite for a good one. In this case one exchanges the urge to view pornography for the desire to listen to spirit-filled Christian messages that promote spiritual growth. Ways to enable spiritual growth includes the studying of the Bible, speaking in tongues, praying, and fasting.

The Principle of Exchanging Appetites can be likened to behavioral therapy for cigarette addicts, that is, the decision to replace their unhealthy smoking habit with exercise or other healthful behavior. The major difference is the grace and assistance of the Holy Spirit in the exchange of the urge to view pornography for the desire to listen to Christian messages.

2. The Principle of Regulating the Use of Social Media

Since the invention of social media, the world has become exposed to a great amount of public nudity, which is becoming normal. As our privacy is becoming extinct, we are increasingly exposed to unsolicited sexually explicit content. As an individual, however, you possess some self-control. You have the power to stay away from pornographic sites, to be selective about social media apps, and delete apps that promote sexually immorality.

Several social media apps let users personalize their control settings and limit content according to their individual preferences. This includes blocking, removing tags, muting, unfollowing, unfriending, and installing ad blockers. You can limit the category of friends you add to your social media platforms and the kind of content you view. Several social media apps now suggest contents, people to follow, ads, and feeds based on the kinds of content viewers follow and watch.

3. The Principle of Discarding Pornographic Material

Whatever the human soul sees with the eye and hears with the ear has the potential to leave an indelible mark. Satan usually tempts people by using the ungodly things they desire or have come in contact with. A person seeking deliverance from pornography must first discard every form of pornographic material they have to show their readiness to God. Those delivered from the addiction of pornography must make sure never to obtain pornographic materials again. When a person previously delivered from addiction to pornography reacquires such materials, Satan takes advantage of idle moments. He uses these moments to instill sexually immoral thoughts and reuse these materials to bring about his victim's backsliding into sexual sin. You must guard your eyes and turn them away from ungodly things. As the Psalmist says: *"Turn my eyes from looking at worthless things; and give me life in your ways." Psalm 119:37 (ESV)*

4. Genuine Heart-Prayer Cry

When viewing pornography becomes uncontrollable, it is a sign that a demon is involved. Praying to God authorizes Him to intervene and drive the demons away. When we pray, God searches our heart to find our motives and intentions. He knows if you are serious about your prayers for deliverance or only praying so you can say you prayed. God watches to see if you will play your part by throwing away all the objects that led you to sin. You cannot pray for help and then maintain an interest in the items that were conducive to your sinning. It is your responsibility to block pornographic sites while God provides the grace that will enable you never to look for a reason to return.

Your prayers arise to God like incense. They can also be an abomination if you pray while conscious of your sin. God can deny selfish and opportunistic prayers. People who communicate with God only when they need something, but do not care to know what God needs from them, are selfish. God is constantly searching for people who can carry out kingdom duties and assignments on earth. As Jesus said, as recorded in the *Book of Matthew: "Then he said to his disciples, 'The harvest is plentiful but the workers are few. Ask the lord of the harvest, therefore, to send out workers into his harvest field.'"* Matthew 9:37-38 (NIV)

You can only know what God desires of you when you are in constant communion and intimacy with Him. The *Book of John reveals this reward: "If you remain in Me and My words remain in you, ask whatever you wish, and it will be done for you."* John 15:7 (BSB)

Another reason why God might deny prayer requests is because they are filled with empty talk. If your prayers do not move you, they will not move God. *"Surely God will not listen to empty talk, Nor will the Almighty regard it."* Job 35:13 (NKJV)

Sometimes God waits for us to break through a level of prayer to experience a different dimension of Him before He answers. A promise made in His presence moves Him to act. The *Book of 1 Samuel* records that Hannah, the mother of Samuel, was barren for a long time. God answered her prayers for a son after she decided to make a vow to Him (1 Samuel 1:9-18). Another person who went the extra mile in his prayer request was Bartimaeus, the blind man, as recorded in the *Book of Mark*. Hearing that Jesus was passing through his city, Bartimaeus took advantage of that opportunity. He screamed for help so loudly that people nearby asked that he be quiet. But that only made him scream more. Jesus restored his sight (Mark 10:46-52). These true stories encourage us to increase the intensity of our prayers whenever we do not see the results that we desire.

> *Once after a sacrificial meal at Shiloh, Hannah got up and went to pray. Eli the priest was sitting at his customary place beside the entrance of the Tabernacle. Hannah was in deep anguish, crying bitterly as she prayed to the Lord. And she made this vow: "O Lord of Heaven's Armies, if you will look upon my sorrow and answer my prayer and give me a son, then I will give him back to you. He will be yours for his entire lifetime, and as a sign that he has been dedicated to the Lord, his hair will never be cut. As she was praying to the Lord, Eli watched her. Seeing her lips moving but hearing no sound, he thought she had been drinking. "Must you come here drunk?" he demanded. "Throw away your wine!" "Oh no, sir!" she replied. "I haven't been drinking wine or*

anything stronger. But I am very discouraged, and I was pouring out my heart to the Lord. Don't think I am a wicked woman! For I have been praying out of great anguish and sorrow." "In that case," Eli said, "go in peace! May the God of Israel grant the request you have asked of him." "Oh, thank you, sir!" she exclaimed. Then she went back and began to eat again, and she was no longer sad. 1 Samuel 1:9-18 (NLT)

Then they came to Jericho. As Jesus and his disciples, together with a large crowd, were leaving the city, a blind man, Bartimaeus (which means "son of Timaeus"), was sitting by the roadside begging. When he heard that it was Jesus of Nazareth, he began to shout, "Jesus, Son of David, have mercy on me!" Many rebuked him and told him to be quiet, but he shouted all the more, "Son of David, have mercy on me!" Jesus stopped and said, "Call him." So they called to the blind man, "Cheer up! On your feet! He's calling you." Throwing his cloak aside, he jumped to his feet and came to Jesus. "What do you want me to do for you?" Jesus asked him. The blind man said, "Rabbi, I want to see." "Go," said Jesus, "your faith has healed you." Immediately he received his sight and followed Jesus along the road. Mark 10:46-52 (NIV)

5. <u>The Principle of Avoiding Movies with Intense Sexual Activity or Fast-forwarding through Scenes with Nudity</u>

Nudity and sex scenes in movies have become glorified. They corrupt innocent minds and adversely affect the wider society. When movie celebrities take sexual roles, their social prestige is transferred to the evil acts they portray, thereby making them seem good in the eyes of their audience. Fortunately, there are more Christians today creating and promoting godly movies.

A movie's effect goes beyond the entertainment it provides. It extends to the shaping of the mindset, standards, and behavior of individuals it entertains. Viewing sexual scenes imprints the soul and provides a foothold for a spirit spouse to gain entry. This imprint is evident in the sexual dreams the moviegoer has. It is thus advisable for the unmarried to avoid movies with an extreme amount of sex scenes. If you can't avoid watching a movie, cover your eyes. Or, if you're watching a recording, fast forward through those scenes.

6. <u>The Principle of Parental Guidance and Control</u>

Parents have a major role to play in protecting their children from exposure to pornography. One reason for the increase in the viewing of pornographic contents by teenagers is the lack of parental guidance and control. As we read in the *Book of* Proverbs: *"Those who spare the rod of discipline hate their children. Those who love their children care enough to discipline them." Proverbs 13:24 (NLT)*

There are different kinds of rods of discipline. In the case of the regulation of online and social media content for children, do not spare the rod. Providing everything your children desire does not prove you love them. They must wait until they attain a certain level of maturity before you give them some-things they want. God, our father, also uses this approach in His dealings with us, His children. Be intentional in blocking pornographic contents on their devices and restrict social media apps. Regulate the cartoons or programs they watch. Be mindful of the friends they keep. Engage in conversation with them. Let them know why you are taking certain mea-sures. Explain to them the war between the kingdom of dark-ness and the kingdom of light. Get to know their friends. Use web filters and install ad blockers. Restrict the movies they watch and restrict the gaming apps they use. Since children take to observational learning, you must ensure they are not imitating the ungodly behaviors they watch.

7. Deliverance

Most people who struggle with pornography addiction expe-rience it as a result of demonic interference and manipulation. Before pornography addicts can successfully implement the solutions offered in this book, they must first undergo deliv-erance. Some will require deliverance with the help of a Christian deliverance minister, and some will need self-deliv-erance prayers. For self-deliverance prayers, see Appendix 1: Prayers of Deliverance from Pornography.

Chapter 3:

FORNICATION (PREMARITAL SEX)

S ex was created by God for procreation and recreation between one man and one woman who are married to each other. If enjoyed under the rightful condition of marriage, it will earn God's approval and blessings, but under the wrong conditions, His reproach and curses.

It has become normal for people to engage in sexual immorality, such as fornication, without any feeling of guilt. Society glorifies this ungodly act, and those who choose not to engage in it are stigmatized as ignorant or weak. Unfortunately, fornication has become rampant among churchgoers. Some preachers downplay or avoid the topic for fear of losing church members. Other preachers do not preach about the social and spiritual consequences of fornication because they, too, are in bondage to the spirit of perversion.

The spirit of perversion facilitates fornication. Even anointed men of God are targets. Most of the time they are "under the radar" of perverse spirits who work tirelessly to bring them down. Never assume that being anointed shields one from sexual immorality. When God blesses a man with his anointing, Satan and his agents are aware of this and begin to surveil him because of the threat he represents to the kingdom of darkness. As the Psalmist says: *"You prepare a table before me in the presence of my enemies; You anoint my head with oil; My cup runs over." Psalm 23:5 (NKJV)*

Great anointed men of God, too numerous to list, have fallen into Satan's hands through the trap of fornication. God may still dwell in the lives of the fallen anointed, but He may reduce the quality of the anointing. God still reaches out to them to get them back on track. Some, however, ignore these attempts of God. They observe the continuing evidence of their anointing, which inclines them to take the mercy of God for granted. This evidence includes the power to heal the sick, raise the dead, work miracles, prophesy, cast out demons, and do mighty supernatural works. The *Book of Matthew* reminds us of their fate: *"Not everyone who says to me, 'Lord, Lord,' will enter the kingdom of heaven, but the one who does the will of my Father who is in heaven. On that day many will say to me, 'Lord, Lord, did we not prophesy in your name, and cast out demons in your name, and do many mighty works in your name?' And then will I declare to them, "I never knew you; depart from me, you workers of lawlessness." Matthew 7:21-23 (ESV)*

The *Book of Judges* gives us an example of a man of God set apart for a season: Samson. God anointed him before he was born to lead His people, Israel. God made him so powerful that he could tear apart a lion with his bare hands. He also caught three hundred foxes, tied them tail-to-tail in pairs, and fastened a torch to them. Samson was so powerful he used a donkey's jawbone to kill a thousand men. God continually used Him to deliver Israel from the hands of their enemies, the Philistines. Unfortunately, Samson fornicated with a prostitute as recorded in the *Book of Judges:*

> *One day Samson went to Gaza, where he saw a prostitute. He went in to spend the night with her. The people of Gaza were told, "Samson is here!" So they surrounded the place and lay in wait for him all night at the city gate. They made no move during the night, saying, "At dawn we'll kill him." But Samson lay there only until the middle of the night. Then he got up and took hold of the doors of the city gate, together with the two posts, and tore them loose, bar and all. He lifted them to his shoulders and carried them to the top of the hill that faces Hebron. Judges 16: 1-3 (NIV)*

Although Samson sinned, God allowed his supernatural strength to remain. God was merciful and gave him other chances. Samson continued in his sins, however, sleeping with a woman named Delilah. He continued his sexually immoral relationship with her, ignoring signs of her disloyalty and betrayal until the spirit of God left Him. Delilah then betrayed Samson to his enemies, the Philistines. They captured Samson, mocked him, and plucked out his eyes. He died without fulfilling his destiny.

> *Then she called, "Samson, the Philistines are upon you!" He awoke from his sleep and thought, "I'll go out as before and shake myself free." But he did not know that the Lord had left him. Judges 16:20 (NIV)*

God only intended sexual intercourse for married couples, but Satan who was cast out of the third heaven, chose to pervert intercourse by introducing premarital (including extramarital) sexual relationships. Sexual intercourse with a spouse or stranger is a form of covenant. As it says in the *Book of Ephesians*: "*For this reason a man will leave his father and mother and be united to his wife, and the two will become one flesh.*" *Ephesians 5:31 (NIV)*

So, when a man and a woman come together in sexual intercourse, they become one in the spirit realm and therefore share the same burden. If unmarried and one of them is being manipulated or tormented by a spirit spouse, the intercourse gives the spirit spouse the legal right to torture them, alter their destinies, inflict them with infirmities, and manipulate them with or without their knowledge.

Sexual intercourse between the unmarried is not the only form of fornication. In the *Book of Matthew*, Jesus gives another example of adultery: *"You have heard that it was said, 'You shall not commit adultery.' But I tell you that anyone who looks at a woman lustfully has already committed adultery with her in his heart."* *Matthew 5:27-29 (NIV)*

Sexual sin begins in the heart, and God will judge both that sin of the heart and the actions that flow from it. Since lusting is considered adultery in the heart, the following are in the same category of sin: "making out" with anyone who is not your spouse, "friends with benefits," "hooking up," touching and stimulating another person's sexual organs, kissing with lustful intentions, and engaging in sex with more than one person at the same time (e.g., a "threesome").

A blood oath or blood covenant is an ungodly practice between two lovers who have decided to engage in sexual immoral intercourse with the intention of securing themselves for each other for future marriage. This involves piercing fingers to exchange blood. Each licks blood off the other and they exchange vows, each promising never to have sexual intercourse with another until death. Others engage a satanic witch doctor (native doctor) who presides over the blood oath-taking. The effect of breaking such a covenant can be instant madness, untreatable sickness, barrenness, impotence, misfortune, or death. Since this act is against the will of God, a demon witnesses it and enforces adherence to the blood oath.

Sexual intercourse with a fiancé or fiancée is a form of fornication that attracts God's curse and reproach and moves Him to withhold His blessings. Satan also takes advantage of this and can inflict barrenness and financial difficulties. You can find other things He could inflict in Chapter 6, in the subsection on the effects of spirit spouse's operation in a person's life. Some engaged to be married say they engage in premarital sex to evaluate their partners' sexual performance and ability to bear children. Others cavalierly engage in premarital sex in the belief that God will forgive their fornication once they're married. These reasonings do not align with the will of God and will give evil spirits enough leverage to tamper with the sinners' lives. Courtship should be a time for the betrothed to get to know each other's likes and dislikes, similarities and differences. It should also be a time to seek counsel, meet members of each other's families, and create partnership prayer schedules. You should set boundaries for yourselves and, if possible, meet in open, public to avoid occasions of sin and other temptations from Satan.

Since marriage is an institution created by God, you must seek God's face before embarking on that journey. If you seek Him with holiness and sincerity of heart, He will make clear whom He has destined for you. There is, therefore, no reason to sign up for dating apps to search for a partner. They do not promote righteousness; rather, they are platforms with an ungodly foundation, directly or indirectly promoting lustful behavior, nudity, hookups, one-night stands, immoral chats, masturbation, exchange of genital pictures, lustful flirting, sexual immorality, fornication, and adultery.

Again, fornication begins in the heart. That is reason enough to guard the heart from evil, whatever it takes: *"For out of the heart come evil thoughts, murder, adultery, sexual immorality, theft, false witness, slander." Matthew 15:19 (ESV)*

The practice of paying to watch people perform sexual inter-course is a terrible sin that ranks with the sin of adultery of the heart because the expression of lust is involved. Fornication has become prevalent in secondary and tertiary school insti-tutions. It is being promoted in the guise "safer sex." Many educational institutions now distribute free condoms and lubri-cants during orientation week, special events, student health fares, and campus clinics. The carnal man might think they are ensuring a healthy sexual environment, but it is actu-ally Satan that has instilled these strategies in the minds and hearts of the leaders to promote the culture of premarital sex. This culture is also responsible for the rise in rape among teenagers.

The effects of rape can be lifelong if the victim does not invite God to intervene. Among those effects are trauma, anger, emotional disorders, anxiety, hatred for parents and the opposite sex, confusion, and suicide. Satan is delighted with rape as a means by which he exploits the victim's situation and finds expression. The proof of his effects is seen when victims become promiscuous and abusive or engage in unnatural sexual behavior. It is therefore important that we denounce rape culture and pray for psychological, physical and, most importantly, spiritual healing of its victims.

CONSEQUENCE OF FORNICATION (PREMARITAL SEX)

1. <u>Alteration of Destiny and God's Plan for You</u>

Satan gains enough leverage to interfere and manipulate the destiny of fornicators. He alters their times and seasons, thereby preventing their breakthrough from occurring. Satan is intentional and strategic about the times he tempts people into fornication. Knowing how much God detests this sin, Satan tempts people when their destiny is about to blossom.

Chapter 39 of the *Book of Genesis* tells us about one of Jacob's sons, Joseph, sold by his brothers to Egypt. There, he served Potiphar, one of the Egyptian Pharaoh's officials. Joseph was well-built and handsome. After a while, the wife of his master asked to have sexual intercourse. Joseph knew this would upset God, so he refused her advances. Later, became the governor of Egypt and helped sustain the Israelites during the seven-year famine. If Joseph had yielded to Satan's temptation and fornicated with Potiphar's wife, he would not have fulfilled his purpose. Many people have left this earth with unfulfilled destinies, while others are in situations that God never intend. The root of this is sexual immorality, specifically the sin of fornication.

2. Delayed Pregnancy (Barrenness) or Transfer of Purpose

Fornication gives Satan the power to control and manipulate a woman's times and seasons. Hating women with a perfect hatred, Satan uses delayed pregnancy or barrenness to inject continuous sadness in their lives. He sometimes even causes a woman's relatives and spouse to pressure her into consulting false gods so that she might bear children. Fornication can move God to transfer the plans he had for one woman to another. God decided in the third heaven that the woman who would bring forth Jesus in human form on earth must be a virgin. If Mary, the mother of Jesus, had lived a life of sexual immorality and fornication, the favor and honor that was to be bestowed on her would have been transferred to another virgin. Whatever God plans to do in a season, He does. If He has destined a person for a kingdom assignment but finds him or her unprepared, He will transfer the grace, favor, honor, and anointing to another. Of course, it does not stop at the transfer of destiny. God's justice system would have to punish the person for his or her sins. As it is recorded in the *Book of Proverbs*: *"Be assured that the wicked will not go unpunished, but the offspring of the righteous will escape."* Proverbs 11:21 (BSB)

To this day, many women who were destined to bear prophets, apostles, evangelists, men of God, freedom fighters, inventors, and world leaders have had their destiny truncated or snatched by Satan due to their engagement in fornication and sexual immorality.

3. <u>Marriage, Delayed or Denied</u>

It is a perverse spirit that facilitates fornication and can make one so promiscuous that one does not see marriage as a gift from God. Perverse spirits can exploit a promiscuous person by exposing the shameful act to the community or society. The one exposed could experience difficulty finding a spouse if the culture of that society frowns upon it. When introduced into one's life through fornication, the spirit of perversion can drive suitors away. These evil spirits can do this either by threatening the suitor in a dream, in the physical realm, or by instilling sudden hatred in the suitor's heart. Another strategy of the perverse spirit is to make the fornicator date the wrong person during the season God has established for him or her to marry. This ungodly relationship becomes a deterrent to the suitor whom God has destined. The destined suitor usually finds and marries someone else. After a while, the perverse spirit allows a split in the relationship. That spirit deprives a woman of her destiny. Now, she realizes that another woman has taken the suitor God destined for her. These perverse spirits steal the breakthroughs, connections, and blessings that come with marriage.

4. <u>Abortion</u>

Abortion is the murder of a human being in his or her embryonic or fetal, and therefore morally innocent, stage of development. Fornication that leads to an unwanted pregnancy is often the circumstance that inclines some to rationalize abortion, a case of one grave sin prompting another. As murder, abortion is a grievous sin against God. Abortion has become prevalent as a result of the immense support governmental organizations provide for it.

Abortion that is procured after sexual intercourse is a selfish, wicked, and evil act that displeases God and invites His wrath. It is hypocritical to see people who would not let any harm befall their pets passionately defend abortion. Every human fetus who dies stillborn or through abortion, whether procured or spontaneous (miscarriage) is taken to the third heaven where God dwells. All partakers in the process of procuring an abortion, be it a doctor, nurse, spouse, parents, family, girlfriend, boyfriend, advisors, fiancé/fiancée, religious minister, and counselors will all share in the guilt and punishment. Abortion can lead to childlessness due to a medical error, a curse, or spiritual attack. This happens because the person who engages in it has given Satan leverage.

Before Jesus died, He promised that the Father would send the Holy Spirit to believers. Today, we enjoy the many gifts the Spirit of God provides the Church. Sometimes the Spirit of God allows believers to experience different kinds of spiritual encounters. Some of them include entrance to the third heaven where God dwells, to see what happens to a fetus after an abortion or miscarriage. Below are some reliable messages that God's servants brought back from their spiritual encounters:

- *There are no babies in hell–***Mary K. Baxter**
- *When the angel of God said, "Come and see," he moved his hand in the air, and a vision of a hospital*

appeared. I saw a woman in the labor room, having a child. The angel of the Lord said to me, "She is having a miscarriage. The baby is only three months old." As I took in the scene, two beautiful angels appeared by her bed. In their hands they held what looked like a basket made of white marble and pearl. It was the most beautiful thing I have ever seen. It opened up in the center and closed on each side. The angels were praising God. I could hear them. When the woman had the miscarriage, the baby's spirit, like a vapor, arose from that little, teeny baby. The angels of God caught it, put it in the basket, closed the lid, and raised their hands toward heaven. The angels began to shout praises to the Lord. They acclaimed Him and extolled Him as King of Kings and Lord of Lords, Creator of all things in heaven and earth. They shouted, "To God be the glory!" **Excerpted from A Divine Revelation of Hell by Mary K. Baxter**

- An angel of the Lord said to me, "From the time of conception, a baby is an eternal soul. If a baby is aborted or miscarried or somehow dies, God knows about it. He has given His angels charge over them. "We bring their little souls to heaven, and God completes them. It doesn't matter if a baby has been aborted or dies naturally. It is fashioned and formed into perfection by the mighty hand of God. "If the parents of these children will live righteously in Christ Jesus, when they come to heaven, they will be reunited and will know their precious loved ones. They will meet them at the gates of glory!" **Excerpted from A Divine Revelation of Hell by Mary K. Baxter** "But," He said with a smile, "I was about to show you the place I made for

My children. I care greatly about all children. I care when a mother loses a child, even as the fruit of your womb, My child, was cast before its time. You see, I know all things, and I care. "From the time there is life in the womb, I know. I know about the babies that are murdered while they are still in their mother's bodies-the aborted lives that are cast off and unwanted. I know about the stillborn and those children who are born with crippling defects. From the time of conception, that is a soul. "My angels go down and bring the children to Me when they die. I have a place where they can grow, learn and be loved. I give them whole bodies and restore whatever parts they are missing. I give them glorified bodies." All over the planet there was a feeling of being loved, a sense of perfect well-being. Everything was perfect. Here and there amid the lush green grass and the pools of crystal clear water were playgrounds with marble seats and highly polished wooden benches to sit on. And there were children. Everywhere one looked, there were children going about all kinds of activities. Each child wore a spotless white robe and sandals. The white robes were so bright they glistened in the magnificent light on the planet. A profusion of color everywhere accented the whiteness of the children's robes. Angels were the keepers of the gates, and the children's names were all written in a book. I saw children learning the Word of God and being taught music from a golden book. I was surprised to see animals of all sorts coming up to the children or sitting beside them while they were in this angelic school. There were no tears and no sorrow. Everything was supremely beautiful, and joy and happiness were everywhere. **Excerpted from A Divine Revelation of Hell by Mary K. Baxter** *There is a pool of water, it's inside made of gold, and children playing in the water. A fish comes out with block letters that says Jesus loves you, the baby reaches out to the blocks and sing to the "Jesus loves you"–* **Mary K. Baxter**

- *Miscarried and Aborted children grow up in heaven, they play music and grow up to the age of maturity, and if their parents leave righteously, the parents will join their children when they come into heaven–* **Mary K. Baxter**

- *A fetus that is aborted even as little as a week will turn into a child in heaven–***Pastor Abraham Yakubu**

- *When the father or mother of an aborted child dies, they approach a place where the aborted child can be seen. The child then gets excited and tells other children that their father and mother are approaching. After which they rush to meet their parents. If their parents repented on earth before they died, their aborted child would be allowed to escort the parent to their final destination in heaven. However, If the parents had not repented before dying, the child will ask his or her parent if the abortion they committed was a good thing. The child's nails will then grow longer, and the child will use it to cut his or her parents. The body of the parent will join back together after being cut and they will be sent to hell–***Pastor Abraham Yakubu**

- *After passing the gate of holiness, parents who have aborted their child will proceed to the city of children. If the parent has not confessed this sin to God on earth, they will be sent straight to hell from the gate of holiness-* **Pastor Abraham Yakubu**

Jesus is ever willing to forgive all sins, including fornication and abortion. To receive His mercy, you must repent and confess your sins to Him. If you want to be saved, please refer to the section of this book entitled, "Four Steps to Receiving Salvation."

DEMONIC INTERFERENCE IN FORNICATION

There are three kinds of sexual intercourse: sexual intercourse with a married partner, which God approves; sexual intercourse with an unmarried partner, which Satan and his demons supervise but God despises; and sexual intercourse by lusting over a person, which Satan and his demons also facilitate, but God disapproves.

In studying the Bible, God's anger towards sexual immorality jumps out at me. We must also react to sin the way God does. It is not enough to love righteousness; you must also hate sin. God has prepared a place for the punishment of fornicators. Defiance of God's law gives Satan and his demons an opening into your life they can exploit. Fornication is ungodly, and Satan and his demons witness it as it is performed and keep evidence of it to prove why they're tormenting, manipulating, and stealing the virtue of the fornicator. There are also angels who record every evil act committed.

Immoral sexual intercourse is one of the easiest means for a demon to transfer from one person to another. This invasion may lead to misfortune, poverty, financial difficulties, barrenness, sexual intercourse in dreams, wasted hard work, perverse and ungodly sexual urges, near-success syndrome, constant relationship breakups, diseases, untimely death, and many maladies.

> It is not enough to love righteousness; you must also hate sin.

FORNICATION: MY STORY

In my quest for heightened sexual gratification, I explored the sins of lust, masturbation, and pornography. I still couldn't derive the sexual satisfaction I desired, so I explored fornication. As my adventure began, I frequented the clubs. The more I went to them, the more uncomfortable I felt. I still could not wrap my head around why others found it fun. I hated the atmosphere, the music, the crowded floors, and the constant fear of fights breaking out.

The clubs were not for me, so I explored online dating apps, through which I found several people ready for one-night stands and hookups. I was able to find dates through the app, and that created a pathway for regular fornication. Each relationship ended quickly, so I was always back to square one. I was not satisfied before, during, or after the relationship. Hardly a day passed without my craving to fornicate.

I measured how good my week was by the number of one-night stands or hookups. I was always conscious about the need to protect myself from sexually transmitted diseases but left my soul unprotected. I always had access to free condoms, and the more I saw them, the more I wanted to fornicate.

> I was always conscious about the need to protect myself from sexually transmitted disease, but left my soul unprotected.

PRACTICAL SOLUTIONS FOR FORNICATION

1. Reading Biblical Scriptures (with Spiritual Trance Experience)

Amongst some of the strategies and solutions that help overcome fornication, I would emphasize one particularly– reading Biblical scriptures. I have encountered a spiritual trance while on my knees praying and in the trance one of my spiritual mentors started speaking of a man who intended to fornicate. He had, in fact, already purchased the means to execute the act (i.e. protection/condoms). However, as he was about to indulge, a scripture he had previously read echoed through his spirit several times. Overwhelmed, he decided not to proceed with his intentions and instantly threw the protection (condom) away. During the spiritual trance experience, I had remembered the time I, as well, threw away the first set of protection (condoms) I purchased while I was still holding on to worldly desires. The message that was sent through the spiritual trance is that reading through Biblical scriptures that condemn the act of fornication and other sexual immoralities is encouraged by God. It is good for you, so you wouldn't fall into the temptation of committing a sin. Reading the scriptures imprints them into one's spirit and resounds by the power of the Holy Spirit in moments of allurement. For some of these scriptures, please refer to "Appendix 3–Bible Passages", especially "Bible Passages on Fornication".

1. <u>The Principle of Running Away or Fleeing: My Story</u>

We must adapt to fleeing or running away from anything that would lead to fornication. Running away means avoiding every occasion of sin, leaving an environment that could potentially lead to fornication. In the *Book of 1 Corinthians* we read: *"Flee from sexual immorality. All other sins a person commits are outside the body, but whoever sins sexually, sins against their own body." 1 Corinthians 6:18 (NIV)*

Since sin brings forth a curse, to engage in sexual immorality is to invite a curse on oneself. Scripture requires you to flee from it. For example, if a friend makes a sexually immoral advance towards you, the biblical counsel is to run away rather than try to withstand such pressure. You do not need to preach or cast and bind any demon. Just flee.

One day, after rededicating my life to Jesus and moving to America, I boarded a New York subway. As I stepped into the subway car, I saw two lovers openly romancing themselves. I immediately left that car and entered another. I took this measure to deprive Satan of an opportunity to tempt me, even though I had already regained my self-control. You must train yourself to get away from situations that can lead to fornication. Never become so confident that you believe you can withstand the pressure of sexual sin if you can just remove yourself from the scene. Remember Joseph, the son of Jacob, whose master's wife invited him to have sex. On one occasion he ran out of the house, leaving his robe behind: *"She caught him by his robe and said, 'Come to bed with me.' But he escaped and ran outside, leaving his robe in her hand."* Genesis 39:12 (GNT)

If the battle was only between humans, we'd have a chance of resisting sexual pressure and fornication without feeling the need to flee the scene. But as we are reminded in the *Book of Ephesians: "For we wrestle not against flesh and blood, but against principalities, against powers, against the rulers of the darkness of this world, against spiritual wickedness in high places."* Ephesians 6:12 (KJV)

We must therefore give room for God to help us. Accepting God's help starts with listening to His commands and paying heed to the escape routes He provides, as stated in the *Book of 1 Corinthians: You are tempted in the same way that everyone else is tempted. But God can be trusted not to let you be tempted too much, and he will show you how to escape from your temptations. 1 Corinthians 10:13 (CEV)*

> Since sin brings forth a curse, to engage in sexual immorality is to invite a curse on oneself.

2. The Principle of Ending Friendships with Sexually Immoral People, Roommates, and Seducers

There are times when God will not use some people until they let go of the bad company they keep. As a Christian, you must use God's wisdom when choosing friends. There are times when God will reveal the real identity of our friends to warn us so that we make the right decision. Sometimes we must end a friendship to prevent falling into the sin of fornication. God is a father, and He expresses His love when He watches over us and warns us of the impending risk of sin. The people we surround ourselves with can affect us subconsciously. You should avoid friends who engage in premarital sex or sexually immoral conversations. Through pressure or peer influence, they can cause you to stumble into fornication.

You must also avoid sexually immoral environments. Be intentional in avoiding buildings, houses, or apartments whose occupants engage in fornication. Hearing a roommate's sexual moans, groans, and panting is a conduit for Satan's seduction of a person into fornication. Sometimes our service to God requires us to make tough decisions. Cutting off friends for the sake of your soul and the kingdom of God might hurt in the short run, but you can always ask God for His grace to get you through the process. We must remind ourselves that whatever we give up for the sake of the kingdom of God is never a loss, but rather a gain. God expects us to make these tough decisions, as He says in the *Book of Matthew: "And if your right hand causes you to sin, cut it off and throw it away. It is better for you to lose one part of your body than for your whole body to depart into hell." Matthew 5:30 (BSB)*

There are many seducers in our society, and many of them are on a mission from Satan. They are skilled at tempting people through their speech, flirtatious behavior, eyes, and bodily movements and gestures. You must also avoid them as much as possible. Finally, you also have the power to remove, mute, and block immoral friends from your social media accounts. In doing these things for the kingdom of God, you must trust that God will send new spirit-filled friends who can assist you in your Christian journey.

> whatever we give up for the sake of
> the kingdom of God is never a loss,
> but rather a gain.

3. The Principle of Avoiding Sexual Immorality While Single, including during Courtship: My Story

Having sex with your fiancé or fiancée is fornication and therefore a grievous sin against God. Sexual intercourse is righteous only between married couples. This principle is both preventive and curative. Curative, in that it shows God your readiness to avoid sexual sin in order to receive deliverance from the addiction to fornication. Preventative, in that it denies Satan leverage to manipulate your personal and marital destiny.

God reveals to His children those whom Satan has planned to use in tempting us into fornication. God can utilize divine encounters, revelations, dreams, and visions to pass on this information to us. He can also tell you, directly or indirectly, to cancel a meeting with someone with a hidden sexual agenda. After I rededicated my life to Christ, I had a friend from Canada wanting to visit me in America. Whether intentionally or not, I sensed that this friend was sent to fulfill Satan's agenda. I initially agreed to host, however, just weeks before the arrival, God warned me in a dream of hidden seduction plans in my friend's travel agenda. Upon receiving two warnings, I decided to cancel the meeting. As a child of God, you must always be on the alert. Do not be like the foolish virgins described in Matthew 25. You are called to the office of a watchman and must therefore be equipped and alert, for the day of accountability approaches.

Be intentional in ending sexually immoral relationships. If you're in such a relationship, tell the person you're breaking up with your reasons. You can tell him or her that you are now born again, and that God forbids fornication. Your godly reason weakens the power of Satan, puts him to shame, and deters your ex-partner from trying to persuade you in the future. Stating your reasons can also reinforce your resolve not to compromise.

66

> You are called to the office of a
> watchman and must therefore be
> equipped and alert, for the day of
> accountability approaches.

4. The Principle of Getting Engaged Only When Ready to Marry

Proposing has become a way to secure benefits—legal, financial, and sexual—and to show responsibility and commitment to another person. Being passionate about marriage is not the same as being ready for marriage, and neither is merely finding someone willing to marry you. Proposing prematurely can be disastrous.

Proposing and engaging is enough to heighten emotions, excitement, and expectations. These are normal reactions a person experiences when they are about to commit to something new. If done at the wrong time, however, the new thing can be a source of negativity. When enjoyed at the wrong time, good things can yield undesired outcomes and so cease to be good. God in His wisdom created times and seasons for human beings, and as His children we must adhere to them: *"And of the children of Issachar, which were men that had understanding of the times, to know what Israel ought to do; the heads of them were two hundred; and all their brethren were at their commandment." 1 Chronicles 12:32 (KJV)*

Premature proposals and engagement can create pressure that can incline a person to commit doing certain things at the wrong time. This pressure can also manifest itself in fornication in order to prove sexual ability, foreplay, sexual intercourse skills, and reproductive ability. But, these are permitted only in the context of marriage.

> Being passionate about marriage is not the same as being ready for marriage, and neither is merely finding someone willing to marry you.

> When enjoyed at the wrong time, good things can yield undesired outcomes and so cease to be good.

5. Marriage

Marriage is a divine institution created for human beings. Sexual intercourse is a gift from God that we may unwrap only in marriage. As it says in the *Book of 1 Corinthians*:

"Nevertheless, to avoid fornication, let every man have his own wife, and let every woman have her own husband." 1 Corinthians 7:2 (KJV)

Marriage serves as a biblical solution to fornication if the marriage partners have self-control. Married people, however, who still feel the urge to commit sexual immorality must seek deliverance, for they have surrendered their self-control to a perverse spirit. Marriage alone will not drive out an evil spirit that motivates a person to cheat, but deliverance in marriage will. Your partner should be enough to provide you sexual gratification.

Getting married late in life is not evidence of maturity or wisdom. We must also learn to see sexual intercourse *only* as a gift from God to the married. Knowing that should incline us not to misuse that gift. When you see a beautiful woman or handsome man, remind yourself that the gift of marriage will someday come to you.

We must also learn to see sexual intercourse only as a gift from God to the married, and knowing that should incline us not to misuse that gift.

6. <u>The Principle of Break-up, Breaking Ties, and Refusing Benefits</u>

Following Jesus Christ requires you to make sacrifices, which can scar and express the testimony of His impact on your life. Although these scars could temporarily cause a degree of pain, they will eventually glorify Jesus in your life by bringing forth peace, joy, freedom, and happiness. Breaking up with an ungodly partner for His sake is one of these potential scars. In fact, it is an initial step to attaining freedom from the yoke of sexual immorality. Breaking up is also a way to break ties and associations. It is a way to refuse benefits that ungodly relationships offer, such as sex and financial help. For example, if you live rent-free with a girlfriend only for the sexual interactions, find another living arrangement. After you've repented from your sins, you must find somewhere else to live. Leaving this situation will give you more time to achieve spiritual maturity. It will also keep you from pressure to commit sexual immorality. It is wise never to trust in your unaided ability to overcome temptation. Instead, trust in the escape route Jesus provides you. Surrender your territory to Him and heed His counsel and wisdom. Only then can you receive strength to overcome the sin of fornication.

7. <u>Prayer</u>

Prayer is a powerful weapon God has given man. It is also a way to have koinonia with God, where He unveils strategies for our daily survival. We must engage in prayer every day: *"Then Jesus told his disciples a parable to show them that they should always pray and not give up." Luke 18:1 (NIV)*

To receive deliverance from addiction to fornication, you must constantly fellowship with God. It is your love for God that motivates you not to sin against Him. You must also pray to sustain the deliverance received. God sometimes rewards those who have developed genuine relationships with Him and have overcome this addiction by giving them the anointing to teach and minister deliverance to others. No time spent in the presence of God is wasted. You might observe among Christians that some anointed with the healing grace were always sick when they were young, or a person who preaches faith was once timid. Sometimes it is their original destiny to work in this grace and anointing, but Satan attacks them early so that they deviate from their path and never enter into their divine calling.

God can leave some prayers unanswered. One reason for this is the unforgiveness of the person praying. Before God can hear your prayer, He must forgive you. But before He forgives you, you must forgive others no matter how much hurt you feel. As Jesus says:

> And when you stand praying, if you hold anything against anyone, forgive them, so that your Father in heaven may forgive you your sins. Mark 11:25-26 (NIV)

> Forgive us the wrongs we have done as we ourselves release forgiveness to those who have wronged us. Matthew 6:12 (TPT)

> For if you forgive other people when they sin against you, your heavenly Father will also forgive

you. But if you do not forgive others their sins, your Father will not forgive your sins. Matthew 6:14-15 (NIV)

Deliverance from the spirit of perversion that facilitates fornication is received through God's mercy. To obtain His mercy, which we do not deserve, we must be reasonable in showing gratitude and readiness by forgiving all who have wronged us. Forgiving can be difficult for some, but the grace to make it easy is available when you ask Holy Spirit for it. It is good to show mercy to those who do not deserve it, just as Jesus has done for us.

Another time prayer is not answered is when people look away from the needy, the sick, the hungry and the thirsty, strangers, and prisoners. Jesus regards these people as Himself. So, whatever you do to *them* is also done to *Him*. The *Book of Matthew* states:

Then he will say to those on his left, "'Depart from me, you who are cursed, into the eternal fire prepared for the devil and his angels. For I was hungry and you gave me nothing to eat, I was thirsty and you gave me nothing to drink, I was a stranger and you did not invite me in, I needed clothes and you did not clothe me, I was sick and in prison and you did not look after me." They also will answer, "Lord, when did we see you hungry or thirsty or a stranger or needing clothes or sick or in prison, and did not help you?" He will reply, "Truly I tell you, whatever you did not do for one of the least of these, you did not do for me." Matthew 25:41-44 (NIV)

God also rejects the prayers of those who ignore the cries of the poor, as written in the book of Proverbs: *"Whoever shuts their ears to the cry of the poor will also cry out and not be answered." Proverbs 21:13 (NIV)*

If you have prayed fulfilling all God's requirements in holiness and righteousness, then be assured that your prayers have been heard and will be answered. You must have faith and confidence in God. It is the will of God that the oppressed, whether guilty or not, be set free as long as they repent and cry out for help, as recorded in the *Book of Isaiah: "Shall the prey be taken from the mighty, or the lawful captive delivered? But thus saith the Lord, Even the captives of the mighty shall be taken away, and the prey of the terrible shall be delivered: for I will contend with him that contendeth with thee, and I will save thy children." Isaiah 49: 24-25 (KJV)*

> No time spent in the presence of God is wasted.

> It is good to show mercy to those who do not deserve it, just as Jesus has done for us.

8. <u>The Principle of Adaptability through Long-term Sexual Abstinence</u>

Once a person abstains from an activity for a long time, without external influence, interest in it weakens. This principle is evident in various areas of life but is advantageous in combating fornication. Long-term abstinence from sex can lower sexual interest, urge, and cravings. The craving for sex will die a natural death, thereby freeing the flesh to submit to the spirit. An unmarried individual has no business establishing a sexual relationship with anyone. Sexual abstinence should be a part of your default setting until marriage. If a person decides to abstain from fornication and then focuses on something else, his or her craving for sexual intercourse will fade. This happens because it is no longer constantly on their minds. The ability to abstain from sexual intercourse is possible. There are widows, who lose interest in remarriage or sexual activities after losing their spouses. One reason for this is that they've redirected their focus and attention to other matters, like the welfare of their children or work. All human beings have the ability to abstain from fornication. Spirit-filled Christians, however, receive special assistance through the Holy Spirit, as it says in the *Book of 2 Timothy: "For God will never give you the spirit of fear, but the Holy Spirit who gives you mighty power, love, and self-control." 2 Timothy 1:7 (TPT)*

During your journey to abstinence from fornication, find Jesus. He's the reason you make the sacrifices.

9. <u>The Principle of Rechanneling the Pain of a Breakup</u>

It has become common for young people who have gone through a relationship break-up to head immediately to the clubs, brothels, parties, or other ungodly social gatherings. They do this for several reasons: they seek comfort, sympathy, and a person ready for a one-night stand in order to spite their ex. Usually this only worsens their situation, bringing with it more emptiness, sadness, and even the potential of being raped. There are, however, other people who visit these places only to find opportunities to engage in sexual immorality with those who have recently experienced a relationship breakup, thus exploiting their weakness. They achieve this by showing false sympathy and playing the victim with alcohol, just to take advantage of his or her situation.

Handling a breakup by replacing one sexually immoral partner with another is a sign of ignorance. The break-up should be seen as an opportunity to repent from sexual immorality and draw closer to God. Sometimes God permits such situations to occur in order to get people's attention so they can discover their destiny. The road to your true destiny starts with Jesus, and not your sexual immoral partner. As the *Book of John* says:

> *"Jesus answered, 'I am the way and the truth and the life. No one comes to the Father except through me.'" John 14:6 (NIV)*

> The road to your true destiny starts with Jesus, and not your sexual immoral partner.

The proof that you have found Jesus lies in the forgiveness you extend to your ex and the peace you receive from Christ. Do not give malice or anger any room in your life. At the end of every break-up, Jesus knocks again at the door of your heart. If you pay attention, you'll hear His voice. Open the door, and He will come in and stay with you forever. His presence is peace and love. In the *Book of Revelation* we read: *"Behold, I stand at the door and knock. If anyone hears my voice and opens the door, I will come in to him and eat with him, and he with me." Revelation 3: 20 (ESV)*

Here is advice for those going through the break-up of a sexually immoral relationship:

- Avoid staying idle.
- Exercise more.
- Study the Scriptures.
- Read more spirit-filled Christian books.
- Make new spirit-filled Christian friends.
- Never beg your ex to come back.
- Travel more, if you can.
- Be more engaged in church activities.
- Listen to more spirit-filled Christian audio and videos about letting go and other topics that spur spiritual growth.

- Seek counselling from a spirit-filled Christian counselor.
- Invest in yourself.
- Do not reestablish contacts with sexually immoral partners until complete healing takes place.
- Purchase or adopt a pet.
- Explore your skills.
- Take up a hobby.
- Pray more.
- Try not to be sad.
- Let the healing process take its course.

If you are genuine during this journey and promise never to return to your sexually immoral past, you will find Jesus along the way.

10. The Principle of Limiting Contact with People You've Lusted Over

The buildup of lust over time paves way for fornication. The principle of limiting contact with people you once lusted over or continue to do so aims at providing a quick and temporary escape route. It provides you a way out rather than withstand the internal pressure. Limiting such interactions extends to online platforms: avoid chatting or video-calling so as not to put yourself in a situation where your flesh can find expression, especially when you know the other person is immorally inclined. You can invoke this principle whenever you feel restless, aroused, or suffer a loss of control. This can happen when you see a sexually attractive person. By doing this, you can suppress the compulsion to flirt or establish immoral sexual contacts.

11. <u>The Principle of Discarding Sexual Materials if Not Married</u>

The sight of sexual materials can be enough to incite one to fornicate. What we see has the potential to influence our actions and corrupt our minds. If you are unmarried, you cannot claim to desire deliverance from the addiction of fornication or claim to be sustaining your deliverance from it if you still possess condoms and other sexual objects. Just the same way, you cannot claim to love righteousness and also harbor evil. Keeping these items can be likened to giving a murderer (Satan) the knife he would use to stab you. The more you see such items, the more you provide materials for Satan to use to lure and tempt you. It is therefore in your best interest to discard all such items if you not married. Their presence can never initiate righteous thoughts. For example, a condom is always associated with sexual intercourse, and your mind will process nothing else when you see it.

12. <u>The Principle of Parental Vigilance</u>

Parents have a major role to play in protecting their children from exposure to things that may encourage their engagement in premarital sex. As parents, you must never engage in sexual intercourse where your children can see you. Be discreet, for children are inquisitive and observational learners. Their observation of you in your intimacy can inspire them to research and replicate the act with classmates, friends, and siblings. This can pollute their souls. You must therefore restrict what they watch, what they listen to, who can shower with them, and where they may go on holiday or vacation. If you want to protect your children's innocence, you must be extra vigilant. As we read in the *Book of 1 Peter*: *"Stay alert! Watch out for your great enemy, the devil. He prowls around like a roaring lion, looking for someone to devour."* *1 Peter 5:8 (NLT)*

Many children who experience one or another form of sexual assault become promiscuous. Their experience is an unfortunate weed that Satan plants in their lives. As it says in the *Book of Matthew*: *"But while everyone was sleeping, his enemy came and sowed weeds among the wheat, and went away."* *Matthew 13:25 (NIV)*

It is therefore your responsibility to cover your children with prayers and teach them how to engage in spiritual battles so that God's angels can engage in their physical battles.

13. Deliverance

Once you can no longer control your engagement in a sexual act by sheer will, it is a sign that an evil spirit has taken charge of at least some of your faculties. This applies to fornication. The way forward is to engage in deliverance, either through a Christian minister or your self-deliverance prayers. For self-deliverance prayers please refer to Appendix 1: Prayers of Deliverance from Fornication.

Chapter 4:

LUST

Lust is a perverse sexual craving that utilizes all five human senses (hearing, touching, smelling, taste, and sight), the mind, and its cognitive processes. It is a strong craving that needs to either be satisfied or quenched. Lust can be likened to a rushing stream of water. Unhindered, the stream can burst its boundaries and lead to extreme damage. The human imagination is the tool most exploited in this process. Imagination by itself is not sinful: God created it for our use in glorifying Him. What is a sin, however, is sexually immoral ideation, that is, conjuring up in your mind sexual acts with anyone other than your spouse; that's lust. It is Satan's desire to pervert everything God has created. He makes them turn from their natural state to an unnatural and perverse state.

Lust aims to go beyond the sexually immoral imaginative state to the heart, so that the person who lusts carries out whatever was imagined. Lust has a mechanism of expression that starts with the five senses. One or more sense is then used to send a signal, a thought, to the mind. The imaginative and emotional aspects of the human being are also utilized. If the practice of lust takes place for a long time, the heart becomes contaminated with sin. The heart is the chief aspect needed for lust to find expression. One demonstrates full expression of lust by practicing the imagined sexually immoral act. The *Book of Matthew* says: "*For out of the heart come evil thoughts, murder, adultery, sexual immorality, theft, false witness, slander.*" *Matthew 15:19 (ESV)*

The real intention of Satan is that the expression of sexual sin ultimately leads to death and eternal damnation. As it says in the *Book of Romans*: "*For the wages of sin is death, but the gift of God is eternal life in Christ Jesus our Lord.*" *Romans 6:23 (NKJV)*

> LUST = 5 senses (sight, hearing, touch, smell, taste) → Mind (Brain / Cognitive process) → Heart → Expression through sexual immorality → Death → Eternal Damnation (Hell)

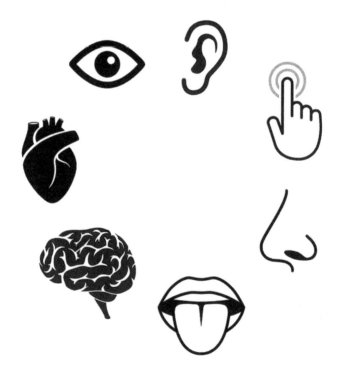

In the *Book of Matthew*, we also find the connection between lust, the heart, and sexual immorality; in this case, adultery. Lust craves to be satisfied through sexual sin: *"But I tell you that anyone who looks at a woman lustfully has already committed adultery with her in his heart." Matthew 5:28 (NIV)*

Lust craves for satisfaction like an opiate; when it is fed with what it desires, its craving becomes stronger. If a person watches pornography to satisfy their lust, at some point it is no longer enough to bring gratification. He or she will then turn to another, stronger means to derive the same gratification, such as masturbation. Fornication and other forms of sexual immorality will soon follow. It is a cycle that never ends with any true contentment. Lust must be nipped in the bud or become uncontrollable. Its effects always bring disastrous consequences, as we see in the life of the son of King David:

> *Some time passed. David's son Absalom had a beautiful sister named Tamar, and David's son Amnon was infatuated with her. Amnon was frustrated to the point of making himself sick over his sister Tamar because she was a virgin, but it seemed impossible to do anything to her. Amnon had a friend named Jonadab, a son of David's brother Shimeah. Jonadab was a very shrewd man, and he asked Amnon, "Why are you, the king's son, so miserable every morning? Won't you tell me?" Amnon replied, "I'm in love with Tamar, my brother Absalom's sister." Jonadab said to him, "Lie down on your bed and pretend you're sick. When your father comes to see you, say to him, 'Please let my sister Tamar come and give me*

something to eat. Let her prepare a meal in my presence so I can watch and eat from her hand.'" So Amnon lay down and pretended to be sick. When the king came to see him, Amnon said to him, "Please let my sister Tamar come and make a couple of cakes in my presence so I can eat from her hand." David sent word to Tamar at the palace: "Please go to your brother Amnon's house and prepare a meal for him." Then Tamar went to his house while Amnon was lying down. She took dough, kneaded it, made cakes in his presence, and baked them. She brought the pan and set it down in front of him, but he refused to eat. Amnon said, "Everyone leave me!" And everyone left him. "Bring the meal to the bedroom," Amnon told Tamar, "so I can eat from your hand." Tamar took the cakes she had made and went to her brother Amnon's bedroom. When she brought them to him to eat, he grabbed her and said, "Come sleep with me, my sister!" "Don't, my brother!" she cried. "Don't disgrace me, for such a thing should never be done in Israel. Don't commit this outrage! Where could I ever go with my humiliation? And you—you would be like one of the outrageous fools in Israel! Please, speak to the king, for he won't keep me from you." But he refused to listen to her, and because he was stronger than she was, he disgraced her by raping her. So Amnon hated Tamar with such intensity that the hatred he hated her with was greater than the love he had loved her with. "Get out of here!" he said. "No," she cried, "sending me away is much worse than the great wrong you've already done to me!" But he refused to listen to her. Instead, he called to the servant who waited on him, "Get this away from me, throw her out, and bolt the door behind her!" Amnon's servant threw her out and bolted the door behind her. Now Tamar was wearing a long-sleeved robe, because this is what the king's virgin daughters wore. Tamar put ashes on her head and tore the long-sleeved robe she was wearing. She put her hand on her head and went away crying out. Her brother Absalom said to her, "Has your brother Amnon been with you? Be quiet for now, my sister. He is your brother. Don't take this thing to heart." So Tamar lived as a desolate woman in the house of her brother Absalom. When King David heard about all these things, he was furious. Absalom didn't say anything to Amnon, either good or bad, because he hated Amnon since he disgraced his sister Tamar. Two years later, Absalom's sheepshearers were at Baal-hazor near Ephraim, and Absalom invited all the king's sons. Then he went to the king and said, "Your servant has just hired sheepshearers. Will the king and his servants please come with your servant?" The king replied to Absalom, "No, my son, we should not all go, or we would be a burden to you." Although Absalom urged him, he wasn't willing to go, though he did bless him. "If not," Absalom said, "please let my brother Amnon go with us." The king asked him, "Why should he go with you?" But Absalom urged him, so he sent Amnon and all the king's sons. Now Absalom commanded his young men, "Watch Amnon until he is in a good mood from the wine. When I order you to strike Amnon, then kill him. Don't be afraid. Am I not the one who has commanded you? Be strong and valiant!" So Absalom's young men did to Amnon just as Absalom had commanded. Then all the rest of the king's sons got up, and each fled on his mule. While they were on the way, a report reached David: "Absalom struck down all the king's sons; not even one of them survived!" In response the king stood up, tore his clothes, and lay down on the ground, and all his servants stood by with their clothes torn. But Jonadab, son of David's brother Shimeah, spoke up: "My lord must not think they have killed all the young men, the king's sons, because only Amnon is dead. In fact, Absalom has planned this ever since the day Amnon disgraced his sister Tamar. So now, my lord the king, don't take seriously the report that says all the king's sons are dead. Only Amnon is dead." Meanwhile, Absalom had fled. When the young man who was standing watch looked up, there were many people coming from the road west of him from the side of the mountain. Jonadab said to the king, "Look, the king's sons have come! It's exactly like your servant said." Just as he finished speaking, the king's sons entered and wept loudly. Then the king and all his servants also wept very bitterly. But Absalom fled and went to Talmai son of Ammihud, king of Geshur. And David mourned for his son every day. After Absalom had fled to Geshur and had been there three years, King David longed to go to Absalom, for David had *finished grieving over Amnon's death. 2 Samuel 13: 1-39 (CSB)*

We can infer from this true story that lust is not love. It is a strong, temporary, perverse passion that only leads to sin and punishment. In fact, the person who lusts often ends up developing a sudden hatred towards the person they lusted over immediately after being sexually gratified by that person. Have you ever experienced music playing in your mind as you are about to wake up from sleep? The conduit of the sound is a route God has created to enable humans to hear angelic songs and heavenly communications. Many people, however, have handed this faculty over to Satan to pervert, consciously or unconsciously. That's why they only hear worldly music as they awake. This scenario recurs with the help of the brain's imaginative component. It was created to give God glory, but some people allow Satan to pervert their capacity to imagine.

LUST VERSUS LOVE

Very often people confuse lust with love. The following table distinguishes them:

LUST	LOVE
Lust seeks the body more than the soul.	Love seeks the soul more than the body.
Lust is jealous.	Love is secure.

Lust is sponsored by Satan.	Love is sponsored by God.
Lust is a temporary desire that ends once the urge is quenched.	Love is long-lasting.
Lust is envious, boastful, and proud; dishonors others, is self-seeking, easily angered, keeps a record of wrongs, delights in evil (1 Corinthians 13:4-8).	Love is patient, kind, rejoices with the truth, always protects, always trusts, always hopes, always perseveres and never fails. (1 Corinthians 13:4-8).
Lust is conditional.	Love is unconditional.
Lust violates God's principles.	Love obeys God.
The goal of lust is sexual immorality.	The goal of love is not sexual immorality.
Lust does not care about the long-term feelings of the person lusted over.	Love cares about the long-term feelings of the person loved.
Lust makes a person sick and is full of obsession (2 Samuel 13:2).	Love is patient and brings peace.

Lust is overly concerned with physical appearance.	Love is more concerned about the inner beauty than with appearance.
Lust is selfish.	Love is selfless.
Lust is unfaithful.	Love is faithful.
Lust is an ungodly urge and drive.	Love is contentment and fulfilment.
Lust is controlling.	Love is devotion.
Lust if sex focused.	Love is beyond sex.
Lust is insensitive.	Love is caring.
Lust seeks comfort.	Love makes sacrifice.
Lust is treacherous.	Love is loyal.
Lust seeks pleasure.	Love seeks commitment.
Lust is suspicious.	Love is trust.
Lust yields anxiety.	Love brings peace.
Lust is inconsiderate.	Love is thoughtful.
Lust wants premarital sex and sexual immorality.	Love wants marriage.
Lust comes from the flesh.	Love comes from the heart.

Lust is proud.	Love is humble.
Lust destroys.	Love protects.
Lust keeps grudges.	Love forgives.
Lust has no self-control.	Love has self-control.
Lust is quick to remember the wrongs of the past.	Love is quick to forget the wrongs of the past.
Lust abandons.	Love stays.
Lust uses.	Love invests.
Lust is stingy.	Love is generous.
Lust is insecure among the family and friends of partner.	Love wants to meet family and friends of a partner.
Lust is insensitive.	Love is considerate.
Lust makes a person sick.	Love is healthy.

PRACTICAL SOLUTIONS TO THE PROBLEM OF LUST

1. The Principle of Redirecting or Rechanneling of Thoughts

The more intense a perverse sexual craving, the greater is the effort required to satisfy it. A married person can easily satisfy a sexual craving by engaging, or redirecting all sexual imaginings to his or her spouse. Unmarried individuals should redirect all cravings to Jesus. Lust is usually experienced by people who are idle. As earlier stated, lust is like a stream of water. One may use several strategies to control lust, and one of them is rechanneling. Lustful thoughts can be consciously rechanneled to something else. It is better to redirect these thoughts to the imagination of Jesus, His kingdom, God's throne room, biblical stories, biblical parables, and heavenly activities. Redirecting thoughts to Jesus is more effective because of the spiritual effects it leaves on the soul. Lust is a desire of the flesh inspired by Satan. But, with thoughts of God, you can turn away its satanic effect on your soul and mind. This registers in your soul and becomes a part of your defense mechanism. Consider this principle as one of the escape routes God has promised to provide His children. As the *Book of 1 Corinthians* states:

> *No temptation has overtaken you except what is common to mankind. And God is faithful; he will not let you be tempted beyond what you can bear. But when you are tempted, he will also provide a way out so that you can endure it. 1 Corinthians 10:13 (NIV)*

2. The Principle of Blinking

As earlier stated, lust utilizes the five senses as well as the imagination. Some people experience its effects more when they close their eyes to imagine sexually immoral things; others, when their eyes are open. The principle of deliberately blinking can terminate lust. People who experience lust when their eyes are open can opt to deliberately blink for a few moments. Those who experience lust when their eyes are closed can opt to open or deliberately blink. These eye movements interrupt the lust process and prevent people from getting lost in their sinful thoughts. It is also an intentional way to enforce a covenant you can make with your eyes never to imagine lustful things. As stated in the *Book of Job*: *"I made a covenant with my eyes not to look lustfully at a young woman"* *Job 31:1 (NIV)*

3. <u>The Principle of Speaking Back to Lustful Thoughts</u>

Speaking back to lustful thoughts is a way to exercise dominion over them by suppressing them. You can consciously, firmly, and silently speak back to these thoughts by saying phrases like:

> "I rebuke you, evil spirit, who are responsible for these lustful thoughts."'

> "Jesus has prevailed over my thoughts."

> "I have made a covenant with my thoughts not to lust and not to sin against God."

Utter these words firmly, whether silently or with greater or lesser volume. This has a supernatural power and effect that transcends the ear. These words then embed themselves in the brain's long-term memory and then to the heart, where they register. The synchrony between spoken words, the ear, the brain (long-term memory), and the heart will terminate the effect of Satan on your mind and cause him to flee from you. The *Book of James* says:

Submit yourselves therefore to God. Resist the devil, and he will flee from you. James 4:7 (KJV)

4. <u>Speaking in Tongues</u>

Speaking in tongues is a great way to subdue the effects of lust. It counteracts with or distorts lustful thoughts quickly and effectively. As a reaction to lustful thoughts, speaking in tongues gives the Holy Spirit permission to thwart all satanic effects in your soul and remove any satanic residue that remains. These satanic effects include compulsions that make one practice what one has lustfully imagined through masturbation, pornography, fornication, adultery, and other forms of sexual immorality. Speaking in tongues uproots the demonic seeds that Satan plants in the heart of men. It is a unique form of divine communication that Satan and his agents cannot interpret or understand.

5. <u>Fasting</u>

Fasting is a tremendous aid to overcoming lust. It invites divine intervention and brings to God's attention your need for His help. Fasting makes your prayer request stand out to God as we read in the *Book of Ezra: "So we fasted and petitioned our God about this, and he answered our prayer." Ezra 8:23 (NIV)*

Just as fasting cleanses the body from toxins and built-up chemicals, so does it renew the soul, purify the mind, the thought process, and the heart from the effects and residue of lust. Fasting generates both physical and spiritual hunger. It tells God how hungry you are for deliverance and the extent of sacrifice you are willing to make for Him to hear your prayers. In return, the flesh becomes weak, and starves of every lustful appetite. A plant denied water dies after a few days. This is the effect fasting has on lust. During fasting, especially the longer it is practiced, the focus is on God. The person fasting becomes desensitized to all lustful distractions in their surroundings. It is advisable to engage in multiple days of fasting, when seeking deliverance from lust. Some kinds and durations of fast include water fast, fruit fast, and dry fast; 6:00 a.m. to 12:00 p.m., 6:00 a.m. to 3:00 p.m., 6:00 a.m. to 6:00 p.m., and a fast of forty days and forty nights. The effect of fasting will find its way into the mind and heart and recalibrate them to a state of righteousness. The combination of fasting and prayer yields the desired result through faith in Jesus Christ.

6. Prayer

Prayer is a dynamic form of communicating your heart intentions to God. It is a means of inviting God to intervene in earthly affairs. In our lifetime, we will never fully understand the value God places on prayer. There is no limit to what prayer can bring, including combating lust. You must open your heart to God when you pray. Many people feel ashamed to present their struggle with lust and other sexual sin to God. But he is already aware of that struggle and is eager to help, as it is written in the *Book of Matthew*: *"But Jesus looked at them and said, 'With man this is impossible, but with God all things are possible.'" Matthew 19:26 (ESV)*

Not asking God for deliverance from lust is one reason many people continue to struggle with that sin. God wants you to want Him to intervene in your life; not asking Him for help limits His influence in your life. As we read in the *Book of James*: *"You jealously want what others have so you begin to see yourself as better than others. You scheme with envy and harm others to selfishly obtain what you crave—that's why you quarrel and fight. And all the time you don't obtain what you want because you won't ask God for it!" James 4:2 (TPT)*

When we pray but do not see the result we want, we must continue to pray earnestly, having faith in Jesus that He has heard our prayers: *"Pray without ceasing." 1 Thessalonians 5:17 (KJV)*

God's approach to suppressing lust varies from person to person. He might drive away the evil spirit that facilitates lust or direct the afflicted to spirit-filled Christian mentors, books, or audio and video materials that discuss such issues. The latter approach recalibrates the mind, thought process, and heart, and reorients the mindset of individuals, exposing them to techniques they can employ to take control over their thinking.

7. Spiritual Retreat

An individual might be unaware when their lust begins, but at some point he or she will be conscious of it. He or she must decide either to halt the lustful thought process or continue with it. Undergoing a spiritual retreat affects the soul, making a person more aware of when he or she is on the verge of committing. To spiritually retreat from the world is to spend time in the presence of God to reflect, re-strategize, pray, listen to the teachings of God, study the Bible, renew the soul, strengthen the spirit and hear God. A retreat can last days, weeks, or months.

One outcome of a spiritual retreat is the mortification of the flesh and an increased sensitivity to and awareness of sin. You can have your retreat in your home, a hotel room, on a mountain, or anywhere there are no distractions. It is advisable to start your retreat by writing down goals for the retreat, the sins and habits you want God to deal with, and achievements from previous retreats. Try to allow it to last at least three days, eventually working your way up to a week, or three weeks, or as the Holy Spirit leads. If you struggle with specific sins and habits, listen to relevant audio or video recordings.

A retreat is a good time to read Christian books on how to overcome those sins. Make sure to have conversations with God and be ready to hear back from Him. Also make commitments to the ways and means you have decided to use in order to avoid the sins that challenge you, such as the sin of lust. Present these commitments to God, write them down, and ask the Holy Spirit for grace and help in achieving what you ask of Him.

8. The Principle of Controlling Social Media and Deleting Obscene Materials from One's Electronic Devices

As earlier stated, lust makes use of the five senses, including sight and hearing. Social media has played a vital role in our society, but it has also had negative effects. Social media and other online content are conduits of a great amount of obscene material that stimulates lust and inspire people to engage in sexual immoral behavior. Sometimes these materials are unsolicited, but whether they or not, their effects linger long after the exposure. They include audio, video, pictures, posts from friends, or advertisements. It is easy to fall prey to these means of temptation and lust over what one comes in contact with. Premeditation is not required. To remedy this situation, you must use your control settings options. You can install ads blockers, block contents, limit tags, limit comments, unfollow, unfriend, delete and mute pages and social media accounts that expose you to sexually explicit contents. This is how you exercise control over what you watch, hear, and read online, particularly on social media. You should also delete from your electronic devices any pornographic and obscene materials stored that depict friends, celebrities, movie scenes, and strangers.

9. <u>The Principle of Looking Once</u>

It is natural to stare at something one is attracted to. But to merely look at a person, attractive or unattractive, is not a sin. It becomes a sin when the looking generates sexually immoral thoughts. Jesus equated the sin of looking at a person with lust as adultery: *"You have heard that it was said, 'You shall not commit adultery.' But I tell you that anyone who looks at a woman lustfully has already committed adultery with her in his heart." Matthew 5:27-28 (NIV)*

The principle of looking once aims at avoiding lust by resolving to do just that. Suppose, for example, that while driving, you happen to see a sexually attractive person who is also dressed immodestly. If that sight has the potential to make you lust, you must look away immediately. Why? Because the flesh urges you to take a second glance in order to derive ungodly pleasure. You must train your mind to adapt to this form of avoiding lust. To effectively achieve this, you must ask the Holy Spirit for grace. The natural reaction of the flesh is to create excuses for looking twice, but it is within your power to inhibit that reaction. You must take lustful looking seriously, because God considers it a grievous offense, even equating it with adultery. The ultimate goal of this principle is a habit of not staring with lust or otherwise scrutinizing the body of a person dressed in a provocative manner.

10. Deliverance

People who struggle with addiction to the sin of lust may seek deliverance through either a spirit-filled Christian deliverance minister or self-deliverance prayers. In praying for deliverance from this addiction, one must also do one's own part in maintaining its suppression and eradication. That includes the continual retraining of the mind and adhering to the principles discussed above. For prayers of deliverance from lust, please refer to Appendix 1

Chapter 5:

UNWANTED SEXUAL AROUSAL

Once one reaches the age of puberty, one begins to experience sexual arousal to the point of desiring to engage in sexual intercourse. Sexual arousal can occur naturally, but an unmarried person should tame the arousal. As this feeling does not care about your marital status, it is potential gateway to sexual sin if not controlled. Sexual arousal is permitted between people married to each other, because they can satisfy their sexual urges together and lawfully. However, married people must realize that God has only approved their spouses to be their sexual cravings.

At some point an unmarried adolescent will experience moments of unwanted sexual arousal, which can be as the result of hormonal changes. This is the stage where adolescents become more conscious of themselves and the opposite sex. Their hearts beat fast when they see a beautiful woman or a handsome man. Although this could be an unconscious, natural feeling, it must be understood and controlled due to its potential to occasion lust in the aroused person.

When a person becomes controlled by his or her passion, rather than controlling it, it is proof that he or she has turned a natural feeling into a sinful, unnatural feeling. When I was caught up in the things of this world, I experienced moments of extreme sexual arousal. I was constantly aroused, and because it was an urge, I would satisfy it through masturbation, pornography, lust and fornication. But this feeling ended the day Jesus delivered me. (I discussed this in this book's deliverance section in the subsection entitled, "My story of deliverance from sexual sin." Since that day, I have not experienced extreme sexual arousal).

One way to maintain deliverance from unwanted sexual arousal is to replace these thoughts and drives with godly thoughts, prayer, fasting, Bible-reading, and spirit-filled, Christian messages. If your thoughts are of sexual immorality are consistent, you will often experience moments of extreme sexual arousal, unwanted or not, which is not appropriate for unmarried people.

SEXUAL AROUSAL TRIGGERS

Like lust, sexual arousal is triggered through the five senses and other factors. The sense that triggers arousal in one person may not trigger it in another. This problem must be managed with the help of the Holy Spirit.

Sexual Arousal Triggered through Hearing
Sex-related sounds can trigger arousal. A person could become aroused when listening to a conversation about sex. It could even be a discussion that is not related to sex but brings back memories of sexual encounters. Music with sexual lyrics can also arouse a person, as can moans, groans, and/or panting from people having intercourse.

Sexual Arousal Triggered through Sight

Sight is probably the most common trigger of sexual arousal. The eyes are a gateway to the soul and powerful organs that can be used to glorify God, their creator, or Satan. Viewing pornography, erotic dances, nudes, or sexual scenes in movies are means through which the eyes trigger moments of extreme sexual arousal. A shirtless bearded man with strong abdominal muscles can trigger sexual arousal as easily as a bikini-clad woman. The sight of certain inanimate objects can also arouse some people sexually. They all do not have to be godly or ungodly. They can be, for example, red high-heel shoes, underwear (men's or women's), condoms, lubricants, vibrators, and sex toys.

Sexual Arousal Triggered through Taste

You might be surprised to learn that some people are sexually aroused by the taste of certain food, beverages, or other substances. Some foods have been scientifically proven to cause sexual arousal, including aphrodisiacs, such as chili peppers, asparagus, eggs, oysters, almonds, watermelon, and chocolate-covered strawberries. I highlight these foods to inform you, not to tag them as holy or unholy. The consumption of alcohol, traditional herbal medicine, and some drug substances can also cause sexual arousal.

Sexual Arousal Triggered through Touch

The sense of touch and feel can also be an avenue of sexual arousal. The sense of sight need not be involved. The touch of a banana, eggplant, or cucumber can arouse some females. This can happen even when they are blindfolded. For some males, it can be a peach or the inside of a watermelon or cantaloupe. Many people today associate these fruits with sexuality. The touching, groping, or feeling of the human body's erogenous zones, one's own or another's, can also trigger arousal.

Sexual Arousal Triggered through Smell

The smell of certain substances can stimulate sexual arousal. A list of them would include perfume, sex candles, fragrances with aphrodisiac scents, such as cinnamon, vanilla, jasmine, lavender, and black licorice. The human glands in the navels, genital area, and armpit can secrete pheromones, which can arouse members of the opposite sex.

Sexual Arousal Triggered by the Environment

Environmental facts can also set off sexual arousal. Living near, passing by, or going into a club, brothel, or strip club might be enough to sexually arouse a person. The atmosphere of these venues creates the urge to engage in sex. Others associate a motel, hotel, or some residential buildings with sex.

Sexual Arousal Triggered by Hormones

Hormones trigger sexual arousal when they affect sexual desire or libido. They are regulatory substances in the human body (both men and women), and testosterone is one of them. A low amount of testosterone in the male is linked to erectile dysfunction and low sex drive. Other hormones, like progesterone and estrogen, affect sexual desire and arousal in females.

PRACTICAL SOLUTIONS FOR MOMENTS OF UNWANTED SEXUAL AROUSAL

1. <u>Sex in Marriage</u>

Marriage is a unique institution that God ordained for mankind. Sex within the bounds of marriage is effective in controlling sexual arousal and actually satisfies sexual cravings. Although celibacy is a beautiful, commendable, and an honorable state, it is only for people who can exercise self-control. I was an altar server in the Catholic Church, a person who assists priests in the celebration of Mass. We had the opportunity to watch the priests closely and understand the sacraments. I fell in love with the consecrated life of priests and decided to become a priest or monk. My plan was to join the Catholic seminary immediately after secondary school. This interest led to my first angelic encounter in a dream. As I matured and became exposed to the world, my zeal for and interest in the Catholic priesthood diminished and eventually vanished. I then realized that I would need a woman in my life.

As people grow and experience different situations, their passions, needs, and wants might also change. Imagine if I eventually became a priest and after taking my vow and spending years in priesthood, I decided that I was no longer interested in being celibate. I probably would be faced with the option of breaking my vow to God. This is dishonorable and comes with stigma or committing sexual immorality in secret to satisfy my urge which leads to God's judgement. Or, I could continue my priestly journey with regrets. Unknown to me, the time spent in secondary school was a time of thinking over my decision. The decision to be celibate by taking a vow of chastity cannot be rushed. It is my belief that such a decision requires the supernatural backing of God through the release of His grace and that is available through prayers. Apostle Paul wrote: *"Now to the unmarried and the widows I say: It is good for them to stay unmarried, as I do. But if they cannot control themselves, they should marry, for it is better to marry than to burn with passion."* 1 Corinthians 7:8-9 (NIV)

A passion that was never present earlier in a person's life could show up years later. One must consider this factor before deciding for a life of celibacy. There are hormonal changes to consider, due to age or other circumstances. A child who desires to be celibate could change his or her mind after reaching puberty; a woman may decide to live the rest of her life in celibacy after the passing of her husband.

Just as the celibate state is admirable and something to look forward to for those interested in being single, sex is pleasurable and something to look forward to for those interested in marriage. Let the waiting motivate and inspire you to remain holy and free of sexual immorality. As a priest looks forward to the day of his ordination to the priesthood, so should those who are interested in marriage look forward to their wedding day. Virginity is honorable in the sight of God, no matter what the world thinks about it. Sex in marriage would satisfy most of the sexual passions when they arise, so, look forward to marriage.

2. <u>Identify Triggers of Sexual Arousal and Take Steps to Control Exposure to Them</u>

As I discussed earlier, there are many triggers of sexual arousal, some of them ungodly. I advise you to review again the list of such triggers in the earlier subsection. You should also create measures to control or prevent occasions of extreme sexual arousal. Deliverance might be a requirement if you feel they are out of your control. You will learn more about deliverance in Chapter 6 on the incubus (spirit husband) and succubus (spirit wife) and Chapter 7, the section on deliverance. You may also pray the Prayer of Deliverance from Unwanted Sexual Arousal in Appendix 1. Sexual thoughts not expelled from one's mind can also trigger sexual arousal. A person who lusts, masturbates, views pornographic content, or fornicates cannot reasonably expect freedom from unwanted sexual arousal.

Chapter 6:

INCUBUS (SPIRIT HUSBAND) & SUCCUBUS (SPIRIT WIFE)

gnorance on spiritual matters is a strategy Satan uses to subject people to bondage. Some children of God become victims of this: *"My people are destroyed from lack of knowledge. Because you have rejected knowledge, I also reject you as my priests; because you have ignored the law of your God, I also will ignore your children." Hosea 4:6 (NIV)*

Evidence of this bondage includes the presence of spiritual spouses, whose effect are not understood by many yoked with them. The word 'incubus' refers to a spirit husband, a demon who usually appears in a dream with male genitals for the purposes of having sexual intercourse; the word "succubus" is a spirit wife, a demon with female genitals who appears in the dream to have sexual intercourse. Sometimes the spirit spouse can appear in the dream as a hermaphrodite, that is, a being with both male and female sexual organs. Spiritual spouses enter into the life of people through several routes. They can engage in sexual intercourse with their victims without consent in the dream, in the physical realm, and in the spirit realm. Sometimes these spirits can bear evil spirit children for their victims and show them to the people they violate.

These spirit beings gain access to a person's life when permission is granted to them through several routes, direct or indirect, created consciously or unconsciously. But it is the heart desire of God to rescue those under the bondage of spirit spouses, whether their victims are guilty or not guilty of the oppression:

> *Shall the prey be taken from the mighty, or the lawful captive delivered? But thus saith the Lord, Even the captives of the mighty shall be taken away, and the prey of the terrible shall be delivered: for I will contend with him that contendeth with thee, and I will save thy children. And I will feed them that oppress thee with their own flesh; and they shall be drunken with their own blood, as with sweet wine: and all flesh shall know that I the Lord am thy Saviour and thy Redeemer, the mighty One of Jacob. Isaiah 49:24-26 (KJV)*

Here are some of the ways spirit spouses gain access to a person's life:

1. Rape
2. Unnatural sexual practice
3. Seduction
4. Lasciviousness
5. Receiving gifts from demon possessed people
6. Engaging in certain ungodly traditional ancestral dances

7. Adultery
8. Sexual assault
9. Pornography
10. Lust
11. Pedophilia
12. Family blood ties
13. Masturbation
14. Bestiality
15. Familial ties with evil spirits
16. Polygamy
17. Violations of God's law
18. Having sex with multiple partners
19. Satanic rituals
20. Idol worship
21. Generational satanic covenant
22. Unnatural sexual intercourse
23. Relationship blood covenant oaths
24. Marriage to demonic deities
25. Use of materials from the satanic marine kingdom
26. Incest
27. Participation in Voodoo
28. Abortion
29. Prostitution
30. Sexual perversion
31. Sexual immoral kissing
32. Fornication

Many people held captive to spirit spouses have no idea of their presence or effects in their lives. This is because these spirits disguise themselves so that their captives do not expel them through the process of deliverance. Demons (spirit spouses inclusive) do not have bodies of their own.

Constantly desiring to express themselves, they find ways and means to possess the bodies of human beings when they find access. Some spirit spouses do not bother to disguise themselves. Their captives can perceive them in dreams, in the physical realm, or in the spirit realm. Some go as far as to undress their captives when they are asleep and bring the spirit children to their rooms. Sometimes captives wake up with intense sexual arousal, discharged semen, erection, pains in the genital area, or marks that indicate sexual molestation. Some of their victims can smell, see, hear, or feel the touch of these spirits.

Some Effects of the Operation of Spirit Spouses in a person's life

The ultimate agenda of spirit spouses is to steal from their captives, destroy them, kill them, and finally lead them to hell fire. They use several tactics to achieve these goals and can cause the following maladies:

1. Wasted hard work
2. Unhappy marriage filled with quarrels
3. Intense sexual urges
4. Threats from diabolical people in the physical realm
5. Behavioral issues
6. Childless marriage (barrenness)
7. Extreme poverty
8. Threats from human beings and spirit beings in the dreams
9. Demonic spells and curses
10. Inability to find a marriage partner
11. Fertility issues
12. Divorce

13. Miscarriages
14. Death during caesarean delivery of a baby
15. Continuous sexual intercourse in dreams
16. Promiscuity
17. Constant disagreement in marriage
18. Sudden death of fiancé/fiancée
19. Constant illness of children
20. Loss of virtue
21. Pregnancy beyond nine months
22. Impotency
23. Marriage to wrong person
24. Constant sexual arousal while waking up
25. Unexplainable cancellation of marriage plans
26. Habitual masturbation
27. Constant relationship breakups
28. Financial difficulties
29. Delayed marriage
30. Misfortunes
31. Sicknesses and infirmities
32. Wasteful spending of wage and salary
33. Marriage delayed until menopause
34. Sudden hate by fiancé/fiancée or spouse
35. Continuous postponement of marriage
36. Constant unfortunate circumstances
37. Near-success syndrome
38. Untimely death

Step-by-step Solutions to Issues Arising from Spirit spouses
1. Follow the instructions in the section of this book entitled Four Steps to Receiving Salvation, starting with repentance towards God, then faith in Jesus, water

baptism and Holy Spirit baptism. Make sure to say the salvation prayer in that section.

2. Believe that *only* Jesus can save you, and seek Him with all of your heart
3. Throw away all sexual immoral devices you used while masturbating. Delete all obscene pictures of other people on your electronic devices, Including those of your ex-boyfriends, ex-girlfriends, celebrities, and strangers.
4. Break up with every sexual immoral partner (anyone you're not married to)
5. Return or destroy every gift or property received from the person you had immoral sex with, e.g., underwear, clothes, sex tools, jewelry.
6. Resolve never to return to your old ways.
7. Proceed to say the Prayer of Dedication in Appendix 1.
8. Proceed to say the Prayer of Deliverance from Spirit Spouses in Appendix 1.

More on Deliverance from the Spirit Spouse

It is God's desire to set free those under the bondage of spirit spouses. The power to chase these spirits lies only in Jesus Christ. Deliverance can be instantaneous or protracted. God makes the final decision whether to remove these spirits all at once or in batches. God can cast out these spirits in batches, which could bring slight relief to the oppressed. Sometimes God does this so the oppressed can continue praying and, by doing so, building a sustainable prayer life and fasting lifestyle. He uses this opportunity to teach the oppressed lessons and deep mysteries. If the oppressed person is faithful until the end and God is pleased, he or she is anointed to also minister in the field of deliverance.

A single person can be possessed with thousands of demons. An example is given in the *Book of Mark*:

> *They went across the lake to the region of the Gerasenes. When Jesus got out of the boat, a man with an impure spirit came from the tombs to meet him. This man lived in the tombs, and no one could bind him anymore, not even with a chain. For he had often been chained hand and foot, but he tore the chains apart and broke the irons on his feet. No one was strong enough to subdue him. Night and day among the tombs and in the hills he would cry out and cut himself with stones. When he saw Jesus from a distance, he ran and fell on his knees in front of him. He shouted at the top of his voice, "What do you want with me, Jesus, Son of the Most High God? In God's name don't torture me!" For Jesus had said to him, "Come out of this man, you impure spirit!" Then Jesus asked him, "What is your name?" "My name is Legion," he replied, "for we are many." And he begged Jesus again and again not to send them out of the area. A large herd of pigs was feeding on the nearby hillside. The demons begged Jesus, "Send us among the pigs; allow us to go into them." He gave them permission, and the impure spirits came out and went into the pigs. The herd, about two thousand in number, rushed down the steep bank into the lake and were drowned. Mark 5: 1-13 (NIV)*

When Jesus asked the demon-possessed man for his name, the demon responded saying "legion, for we are many." In the Roman army, a legion was a unit of 3,000 to 6,000 men. Therefore, this man had about 3,000 to 6,000 demons in him. The same or even worse could be the case for some people oppressed by spirit spouses. Jesus cast out all the demons at once from this man. Such might not be the case for everyone. For instance, a person could be possessed with 6,000 demons. At their first deliverance phase, Jesus might decide to allow 3,000 demons to leave. As the person persists in his or her prayers and fasting, another 2,000 demons can be chased away. Then at the appointed time, Jesus may send away the remaining thousand. During this praying process, God might decide to open the captives' spiritual eyes and senses to show them mysterious things they might need to include in their prayer. By the end of the process, such a person is set free and has likely reached milestones in the spirit realm they never thought they could ever reach. One of the best approaches to receiving deliverance is to request intercession and a physical deliverance section from a spirit-filled Christian deliverance minister. God might need you to contact a Christian deliverance minister so that he or she guides you in your spiritual journey and growth. This helps because the spirit spouses will respect their anointing and obey their commands. A Christian deliverance minister could also be used by God to tell you the duration of your deliverance prayer and if it needs to be extended. God can also decide to reveal to these ministers the deep mysteries underlying your situation.

In the course of deliverance, you must have sufficient faith and patience. You might not see the result you want when you want it, but you must continue to trust in Jesus and continue praying until the time God has set for your freedom. Spiritual warfare is not the same as physical. Many things go on behind the scenes while you pray. A good example of this is recorded in the *Book of Daniel*. Daniel had been praying for three weeks. He ate no pleasant food or meat, drank no wine. During the days he prayed, he got no response to his prayer. Until the 24th day of the first month, the angel of the Lord appeared and said to him:

> *Do not fear, Daniel, for from the first day that you set your heart to understand, and to humble yourself before your God, your words were heard; and I have come because of your words. But the prince of the kingdom of Persia withstood me twenty-one days; and behold, Michael, one of the chief princes, came to help me, for I had been left alone there with the kings of Persia. Now I have come to make you understand what will happen to your people in the latter days, for the vision refers to many days yet to come. (Daniel 10:12-14)*

God heard Daniel's prayers from the first day he prayed, but warfare in the spirit realm delayed the answers to his prayer, but Daniel had no idea of it. Even though Daniel did not receive any response from God, he continued to pray. Daniel's persistent prayer moved God to send Michael, a chief prince angel, to come to the aid of the messenger angel who was sent to Daniel. This scenario repeats itself in the case of many people who request for deliverance. The Bible states in the *Book of Matthew*: *"And from the days of John the Baptist until now the kingdom of heaven suffers violence, and the violent take it by force." Matthew 11:12 (NKJV)*

Be persistent in your prayers for deliverance. Continue with faith. Do not give up but continue to believe that one day you will be delivered. There is absolutely nothing too hard for God to do. As you pray, make scriptural declarations like the ones stated in the next subsection titled "Scriptures and Scriptural Declarations to use in Warfare against Spirit Spouses." Rest assured that Jesus will deliver you, as we read in the *Book of Luke*:

> *Then Jesus went to Nazareth, where he had been brought up, and on the Sabbath he went as usual to the synagogue. He stood up to read the Scriptures and was handed the book of the prophet Isaiah. He unrolled the scroll and found the place where it is written, "The Spirit of the Lord is upon me, because he has chosen me to bring good news to the poor. He has sent me to proclaim liberty to the captives and recovery of sight to the blind, to set free the oppressed and announce that the time has come when the Lord will save his people." Luke 4:16-19 (GNT)*

The Court of Heaven

Heaven has a court where the hearing of cases and passing of judgements take place. We learn about this in the *Book of Revelation* that Satan appears in that court day and night accusing people (12:10). The blood of Jesus is the most potent weapon in this court, and it has the power to make a guilty captive righteous in the sight of God since it can cleanse all their sins. You cannot argue back with your own carnal wisdom in this court. You must therefore always plead the blood of Jesus Christ and ask it to speak on your behalf. Present every spirit spouse case to this court in your prayers and also plead that God rules in your favor. Ask the Holy Spirit to teach you what to say and present the reasons why you need deliverance: *"'Present your case,' says the LORD. 'Set forth your arguments,' says Jacob's King." Isaiah 41:21 (NIV)*

Support your prayer with psalms and scriptures like those in Appendix 1, the section entitled Deliverance from Spirit Spouses. Warfare prayers are best said around midnight, the hour when demonic operations are most intense. Lastly, you must be patient and have faith, so that you do not fall into Satan's trap. Never be tempted to seek deliverance through diabolic means. There are some cases where people consult with witch doctors thinking they would provide quick freedom from the oppression of spirit spouses. When cases like this reach witch doctors, spirit spouses usually communicate with the witch doctor and there will be an exchange of demons. This is possible because demons operate in cliques. That is, a demon higher in the hierarchy will take charge over the person's case, which might bring about quick, temporary relief. After some time, the person's case becomes worse than it was in the beginning. More demons will then lay claim to his or her soul, citing the broken commandment of God. You will never receive deliverance if you have other plans or options other than Jesus Christ. So, make sure to seek Jesus with all your heart and you will be saved and delivered.

Then I heard a triumphant voice in heaven proclaiming: "Now salvation and power are set in place, and the kingdom reign of our God and the ruling authority of his Anointed One are established. For the accuser of our brothers and sisters, who relentlessly accused them day and night before our God, has now been defeated— cast out once and for all! (Revelation 12:10 TPT)

Scriptures and Scriptural Declarations to use in Warfare against Spirit Spouses."

• **Scripture #1:** Do you not know, brothers and sisters— for I am speaking to those who know the law—that the law has authority over someone only as long as that person lives? For example, by law a married woman is bound to her husband as long as he is alive, but if her husband dies, she is released from the law that binds her to him. So then, if she has sexual relations with another man while her husband is still alive, she is called an adulteress. But if her husband dies, she is released from that law and is not an adulteress if she marries another man. So, my brothers and sisters, you also died to the law through the body of Christ, that you might belong to another, to him who was raised from the dead, in order that we might bear fruit for God. For when we were in the realm of the flesh, the sinful passions aroused by the law were at work in us, so that we bore fruit for death. But now, by dying to what once bound us, we have been released from the law so that we serve in the new way of the Spirit, and not in the old way of the written code. Romans 7:1-7 (NIV)

Prayer Point 1: I once lived in the flesh, now I have been crucified at Calvary where Jesus paid the sacrificial price and so my flesh is dead. The life I live is no longer mine, but the life of Jesus Christ and I am one with Him. So today I declare an end to my relationship and association with you spirit spouses, in the mighty name of Jesus Christ.

- **Scripture #2:** But at night, when everyone was asleep, an enemy came and planted poisonous weeds among the wheat and ran away. Matthew 13:25 (TPT)

Prayer Point 2: In the name of Jesus Christ, I uproot every evil seed that has been deposited in my body at night by any spirit spouse. I recover my virtues from them, and I sprinkle the blood of Jesus on any evil coven that holds my bodily fluid. I am a vessel and the temple of Jesus Christ, so no contamination is permitted in my life. I enter into the merits of the sacrificial death of Jesus Christ and His glorious resurrection. Amen.

- **Scripture #3:** Jesus answered them, "You are deluded, because your hearts are not filled with the revelation of the Scriptures or the power of God. For after the resurrection, men and women will not marry, just like the angels of heaven don't marry. Matthew 22: 29- 30 (TPT)

Prayer Point 3: Spirits are not permitted to engage in marriage or sexual intercourse with themselves or humans. Therefore, it is illegal to be sexually harassed by a spirit spouse in the dream. So, I pray by the power in the death and triumphant resurrection of Jesus Christ, any spirit that violates my body in the dream, spirit, and physical realm, I command you to leave by fire by force, in the name of Jesus Christ.

- **Scripture #4:** If a man marries a woman who becomes displeasing to him because he finds something indecent about her, and he writes her a certificate of divorce, gives it to her and sends her from his house, and if after she leaves his house she becomes the wife of another man, and her second husband dislikes her and writes her a certificate of divorce, gives it to her and sends her from his house, or if he dies, then her first husband, who divorced her, is not allowed to marry her again after she has been defiled. That would be detestable in the eyes of the Lord. Do not bring sin upon the land the Lord your God is giving you as an inheritance. If a man has recently married, he must not be sent to war or have any other duty laid on him. For one year he is to be free to stay at home and bring happiness to the wife he has married. Deuteronomy 24:1-5 (NIV)

Prayer Point 4: Today, I write a certificate of divorce to all spirit spouses interfering with my life and destiny. Let the cross of Jesus Christ be the demarcation between you and me. As I claim back all my rightful possessions in the name of Jesus Christ.

- **Scripture #5:** Do not have two differing measures in your house—one large, one small. Deuteronomy 25:14 (NIV)

Prayer Point 5: Angels and demons have a soul and spirit, while humans have a body, soul, and spirit. The Lord is against sexual intercourse between members of different classes. So, I release the judgement fire of God upon every spirit that has planned to or previously violated me sexually in the name of Jesus Christ.

- **Scripture #6:** Don't you realize that together you have become God's inner sanctuary and that the Spirit of God makes his permanent home in you? Now, if someone desecrates God's inner sanctuary, God will desecrate him, for God's inner sanctuary is holy, and that is exactly who you are. 1 Corinthians 3:16-17 (TPT)

Prayer Point 6: I am a new creature and also a sanctuary of God. No one who desecrates His sanctuary goes unpunished. My body is now filled with the Holy Spirit, I am God's vessel, and therefore I ask you spirit spouses to leave me and face the punishment the Lord has prepared for you in the name of Jesus Christ.

- **Scripture #7:** "'Keep my decrees. Do not mate different kinds of animals. Do not plant your field with two kinds of seed. Do not wear clothing woven of two kinds of material." Leviticus. 19:19 (NIV)

Prayer Point 7: The Lord Almighty has decreed that two different kinds of creatures cannot mate together. So, I draw a line of demarcation with the cross of Jesus between I and you. I also break every covenant, agreements, affiliations, or linkage that has been made consciously or unconsciously with you in the name of Jesus Christ.

- **Scripture #8:** Therefore, if anyone is in Christ, the new creation has come: The old has gone, the new is here! 2 Corinthians 5:17 (NIV)

Prayer Point 8: I have been proclaimed guiltless before the Lord Jesus Christ and I am now made righteous through His sacrificial death and resurrection. My old self is nailed to the Calvary cross of Jesus Christ as I am now cleansed with the blood of the lamb.

- **Scripture #9:** Then Jesus went to Nazareth, where he had been brought up, and on the Sabbath, he went as usual to the synagogue. He stood up to read the Scriptures and was handed the book of the prophet Isaiah. He unrolled the scroll and found the place where it is written, "The Spirit of the Lord is upon me, because he has chosen me to bring good news to the poor. He has sent me to proclaim liberty to the captives and recovery of sight to the blind, to set free the oppressed and announce that the time has come when the Lord will save his people." Luke 4:15-19 (GNT)

Prayer Point 9: Jesus Christ was sent to bring the good news to me, proclaim liberty to me, recover my sight, set me free and announce that the time has come for my salvation. So, I receive the manifestation of all these that God the father prepared for me through His son Jesus Christ. Amen.

Chapter 7:

DELIVERANCE

MY STORY OF DELIVERANCE FROM SEXUAL SIN; OR, HOW JESUS CAME BACK FOR ONE LOST SHEEP

"Suppose one of you has a hundred sheep and loses one of them. Doesn't he leave the ninety-nine in the open country and go after the lost sheep until he finds it? And when he finds it, he joyfully puts it on his shoulders and goes home. Then he calls his friends and neighbors together and says, 'Rejoice with me; I have found my lost sheep.' I tell you that in the same way there will be more rejoicing in heaven over one sinner who repents than over ninety-nine righteous persons who do not need to repent." This parable of Jesus' is recorded in the Book of Luke (15: 4-7).

I was the lost sheep He was looking for and found.

My urge to lust, view pornography, fornicate, and masturbate was still present when I was planning on entering into a new, long-term relationship after a break-up. I had an admirer with whom I had been chatting for a long time, but our greatest barrier was distance. This issue was solved when I moved closer. We agreed to meet, and our conversation quickly led to sexual immorality. This time something did not seem right. The atmosphere was different and weird. I felt disgust, irritation, emptiness, sadness, displeasure, and other feelings I cannot name. I wanted our conversation to end quickly so I could figure out what was wrong. As soon as I was alone, I began to reflect deeply. It was as if my eyes had been opened for me and I could realize all my sins. I felt a deep conviction, a feeling of guilt, even grief. I cried that evening and saw the naked state of my soul. I felt remorse and immediately hated the sin of sexual immorality. I knew deep down that Jesus Christ had removed the yoke of lust, pornography, fornication, masturbation, and extreme sexual arousal. I then felt peace, satisfaction, and joy. My desire for sexual immorality died that evening and my quest for God began.

Several times before this great day, I had made up my mind to remain in sexual immorality because I thought the yoke of addiction to masturbation would never be lifted from me. I thought this sin would follow me for the rest of my life and I would die with it. I was proven wrong that evening: the addiction to masturbation disappeared in a second. Jesus took it away. His lost sheep was found.

The result of my previous quest for sexual pleasure through sexual immorality was *Vanity, vanity, vanity! Vanity of vanities! All was vanity.* I have been fortunate and privileged to know the results of my past actions while I am still on earth. Now you can learn from me that sexual immorality has no advantage. Not everyone will have this opportunity and privilege to realize this while still alive on earth and able to do something about it. Most people will realize this in the furnace of hell. So be grateful to know that sexual sin has no advantage.

As the days went by, a strange hunger to listen to the messages of God welled up inside me. The more I listened to the teachings of Jesus, the more I searched for more of them online. I came across videos of people who had divine encounters and were shown heaven and hell. These videos changed my life. My hatred of sin deepened as my hunger for righteousness increased. The urge to fast, pray, and listen to spirit-filled Christian messages returned. I became a new person, a changed person, as I made progress with God every week. I created a prayer and fasting program for myself and listened to Christian messages that preached against non-sexual sins I had the habit of committing. I threw away all sexually immoral objects in my possession and returned to church. Some of the teachings God used to impact my life at that time were the teachings of Dr. Daniel K. Olukoya, the founder of the Mountain of Fire and Miracles Ministries and also the testimony and teachings of Evangelist Linda Paul Rika, the wife of the International director of Holiness Revival Movement Worldwide. My prayer life changed, my behaviors and life changed, and I became a flame of fire again.

Something interesting began to happen weeks and months after I rededicated my life to Jesus Christ. I started getting messages and chat replies from people I had previously asked to meet up with, the one-night stands or sexually immoral dates I pursued when I was still of the world. They suddenly wanted to meet up. I knew that this was Satan's strategy to lure me back to sexual sin. But unfortunately for Satan, I was already fortified with the grace Jesus gives and the power of the Holy Spirit. I replied to many of them to let them know I was no longer interested in living a life of sexual immorality and that Jesus had saved me. Not all of them, as you might imagine, were happy to hear this. Some cut me off, and I cut some of them off. Months later, I had a revelation in a dream where a demon spoke through the mouth of a witch. The demon said, "we thought you were dead, but you came back like Moses." Satan thought I would be His permanent captive, never expecting Jesus to take me from his hands.

There are many lessons to learn from the stories I have shared with you. What Jesus did for me, He can do for you, right now. As we read in the *Book of* Revelation: *"Behold, I stand at the door and knock. If anyone hears my voice and opens the door, I will come in to him and eat with him, and he with me." Revelation 3:20 (ESV)*

All that is needed from you is to repent of your sins and ask for God's mercy. Be disgusted with your sins and hate them with perfect hatred. Do not become a victim of hell fire. I have heard people say, "Life is short; enjoy it while it lasts." But my response comes from the *Book of Mark: "For what will it profit a man if he gains the whole world, and loses his own soul?" Mark 8:36 (NKJV)*

What shall it profit you if you engage in sexually immoral practices and then lose your soul? Many have gone to bed expecting to wake up the next day but died in their sleep and found themselves in hell. Please take a few minutes to think about your soul in eternity. Where would you end up if you died now? Heaven or hell? Be honest with yourself, and the Lord will help you if you ask Him with all your heart.

You cannot claim to love God and then continue in a sexually immoral relationship. You must treat your body and the body of others as temples of God. Do not desecrate yours or theirs. You are your body's caretaker, not its owner. A caretaker must give an account to his master. The fact that you have no memory of your birth should indicate to you that your body belongs to a supreme being, the Almighty Creator. Heed the words written in the *Book of 1 Corinthians*: *"Have you forgotten that your body is now the sacred temple of the Spirit of Holiness, who lives in you? You don't belong to yourself any longer, for the gift of God, the Holy Spirit, lives inside your sanctuary." 1 Corinthians 6:19 (TPT)*

I felt disgust, irritation, emptiness, sadness, displeasure, and other feelings I cannot name. The result of my previous quest for sexual pleasure through sexual immorality was Vanity, vanity, vanity! Vanity of vanities! All was vanity.

HOW TO KNOW THE SPIRIT OF PERVERSION IS INVOLVED IN SOMEONE'S LIFE

When the spirit of perversion manipulates people, they become unable to control their sexual urges. Any self-control they are able to exercise is a short-term affair. This spirit also manipulates them to the extent that if they do repent of their sexually immoral sins, they soon return to them. Counselling can be a slight help, but not a lasting one, because the person has committed that act so many times, he or she has given up a good deal of their will and self-control to the spirit of perversion. Below is a summary of what was discussed, that is, how one can tell that the spirit of perversion is present in people's lives:

1. *They are unable to control their sexual urges long-term.*
2. *They return to their sins, even after repenting verbally.*
3. *Counselling might have a slight positive effect, but it ultimately fails.*
4. *They experience a loss of self-control.*

WHAT HAPPENS WHEN DELIVERANCE FROM THE SPIRIT OF PERVERSION IS LOST

People can lose their deliverance. This happens when they return to their ungodly lifestyle. Some of them get oppressed again when they refuse to live a life of prayer and intimacy with God. As earlier stated, when God delivers a person from the spirit of perversion, that spirit leaves the body. It then goes to dry places to find rest, but never finds the rest it seeks. According to the *Book of Matthew*, such spirit returns to see if the person's life is vacant and warm. If vacant, the spirit brings seven demons, more evil and wicked than itself, making the person's condition worse.

> When a demon is cast out of a person, it roams around a dry region, looking for a place to rest, but never finds it. Then it says, "I'll return to the house I moved out of," and so it goes back, only to find that the house is vacant, warm, and ready for it to move back in. So it goes looking for seven other demons more evil than itself, and they all enter together to live there. Then the person's condition becomes much worse than it was in the beginning. This describes what will also happen to the people of this evil generation. Matthew 12:43-45 (TPT)

These evil spirits see the people they once possessed as property or territory that they are eager to repossess. And they can succeed in doing so if those lives lack the Holy Spirit. When the Holy Spirit is absent from a person's life, an evil spirit has some authority to control and further dominate such a person. When the Holy Spirit fills a person, however, he only influences them to the extent that the person permits. The Holy Spirit is gentle and does not force its way into a person.

If a person who received deliverance from the spirit of perversion fails to offer his or her life to the Holy Spirit through the pursuit of holiness, righteousness, and spiritual growth, the evil spirit will return with seven stronger, more evil and wicked spirits. Violating the laws of God gives these spirits permission to secure their territory and make the life of the oppressed unbearable. Let us explore the purpose of some of them.

Demon #1: The Spirit of Wastefulness

This spirit of wastefulness allows a person to squander resources on their sin. For instance, a person delivered from the spirit of perversion, which facilitates the sin of fornication, may return to their life of fornication. At this point, the spirit of wastefulness can be invited by the spirit of perversion to entice the captive into spending more of their money on items, such as clothes, underwear, cologne, and sex objects. They may also spend it on prostitutes, at sexual parties, brothels, and strip clubs. The spirit of wastefulness will also move the captive to spend money on people who are engaging in sexual immorality even at the expense of their own family's needs. This spirit makes its captives ignore other urgent needs that require financial support, exposing them to situations where they exceed their budget. Some captives will even borrow money to satisfy their ungodly desires. In the end, they are financially drained. They come to regret their actions, but after a short time they return to them.

Demon #2: The Spirit of Whoredom

The spirit of whoredom the spirit that facilitates prostitution. The spirit of sexual perversion can collaborate with the spirit of whoredom to make a fornicator who lost his or her deliverance transition from sex for pleasure to sex for money. The aim of this collaboration is to solidify the territory regained by the spirit of perversion. They make the captive find prostitution to be an easy way to make money to meet their physical needs, and this discourages the captive from seeking deliverance. The evil spirits provide a double deal to these captives, which is to derive pleasure from sexual immorality and to receive financial gains. These strategies keep the captive yoked in sin and death.

Demon #3: The Spirit of Uncleanliness

The spirit of uncleanliness could be invited to help hold the territory of a perverse spirit after the captive has lost deliverance. This unclean spirit makes the captive crave unnatural sexual desires. The captives then go the extra mile to find ways to please the cravings. At times, this leads them to explore and then get addicted to unnatural sexual behavior. These unclean spirits induce the captives to diversify their sexual interests. It also makes the captive experience hardship while trying to find people with whom they can satisfy their strange desire, so that in the process they become promiscuous.

Demon #4: The Spirit of Fear and the Spirit of Heaviness

The spirit of fear is another spirit that joins forces with the spirit of perversion to re-capture formerly oppressed persons who have lost their deliverance. The spirit of fear utilizes many strategies, one of which is the fear of loneliness. This fear is aimed at making the captive feel continually empty. The captive then seeks relief from loneliness by turning to dating apps, sexually immoral gatherings, brothels, and carnal men and women. This method of combating loneliness exposes the captive to more sins and subject him or her to yokes that only worsen the condition. The spirit of heaviness is also invited to put this captive into a state of depression, grief, and despair.

Sometimes this spirit allows the captives' family and friends to cut ties with them, to intensify their loneliness. Another kind of fear is the fear of re-seeking deliverance. Sometimes the captive can be threatened in their dreams not ever to return or approach the deliverance minister who previously prayed for them. Other captives might experience a strong fear when approaching a church building, or contact a deliverance minister, or attend a Christian gathering.

Demon #5: The Spirit of Rebellion (Witchcraft)

The spirit of rebellion is another evil spirit that can join forces with the spirit of perversion to strengthen its territory whenever an oppressed person has lost his or her deliverance. In the sight of God, rebellion is as sinful as witchcraft and stubbornness as bad as worshiping idols. This kind of sin is common in Christian gatherings and can go undetected. Every authority placed over a person or group of people in the house of God represents His authority on earth. Therefore, they are to be respected and honored. As we read in the *Book of 1 Samuel: "Rebellion is as sinful as witchcraft, and stubbornness as bad as worshiping idols. So because you have rejected the command of the LORD, he has rejected you as king." 1 Samuel 15:23 (NLT)*

What this spirit of rebellion aims to do is to make the captives rebel against God's authority and servants. It can also make them destroy their good relationships and rebel against the intercessors and deliverance minister whom God had used or plans to use in ministering deliverance. One reason this evil spirit does this is to ensure that its captives do not receive deliverance through such ministers. Another reason is to establish a case before God through Satan for why the captives should not receive deliverance. The *Book of Revelation* makes us aware that Satan the accuser of our brothers and sisters relentlessly accuses them day and night before God. Satan presents this case of rebellion to God and other reasons why they should not be delivered. He persistently argues and accuses these captives, day and night before God. *"Then I heard a triumphant voice in heaven proclaiming: 'Now salvation and power are set in place, and the kingdom reign of our God and the ruling authority of his Anointed One are established. For the accuser of our brothers and sisters, who relentlessly accused them day and night before our God, has now been defeated—cast out once and for all!'"* Revelation 12:10 (TPT)

Demon #6: The Spirit of Seduction

The spirit of seduction is another spirit invited by the spirit of perversion to reinforce possession of a territory. This spirit is intentional in its task and goal, which is to keep captives in a continuous state of helplessness. This spirit can make them reach out to re-establish sexually immoral contacts with previous lovers, past crushes, and admirers so they can commit the same sin that once enslaved them. The spirit of seduction can also make past lovers reach out to captives for sexual engagements, even if the captives don't reach out to them. The captives might see this as a great opportunity, unaware that it is but a trap.

Demon #7: The Spirit of Promiscuity and Spirit of Infirmity

The spirit of promiscuity can also form an alliance with the spirit of perversion to recapture a person who has lost deliverance. This spirit makes captives more attached to sexually immoral activities than they had ever been. It can also instill in captives the urge to increase the number of times they engage in sexual immorality. The spirit of promiscuity can also make the captive unsatisfied with one sexual immoral partner so as to make them increase the number of partners they fornicate and commit adultery with. These captives become promiscuous and suddenly want to reach out to past friends, ex-boyfriends, ex-girlfriends, strangers, or anyone who ever made immoral sexual advances to them in the past. Sometimes the spirit of infirmity is also invited to afflict the captive with deadly diseases, in this case, sexually transmitted diseases.

Demon #8: The Spirit of Lack and Poverty

The spirit of lack and poverty can team up with the spirit of perversion to inflict lack and poverty on captives who have lost their deliverance. They allow the captives to experience a terrible poverty where they continually have to rely (partly or fully) on others in order to make ends meet. They can also make the captive rely on sinful means like prostitution for their livelihood to ensure they remain in a constant state of lack. The captive is made to regard human beings as their only source of help ignoring the help and love that God can provide. In other cases, this spirit makes the captive spend all their resources on unforeseen bills that suddenly arise as their payday approaches. Sometimes they spend all their pay on unbudgeted items and borrow even before payday arrives. Some captives might sell their property and spend most of their wages or salaries on medical bills incurred by family members or themselves. The spirit of lack and poverty can also cause mental poverty. The captive lacks ideas about ways to create genuine wealth. These spirits are so evil that they block divine helpers and connections solely for the purpose of keeping the captive in a worse state.

Chapter 8:

CHOICE, SPIRIT, SOUL & BODY

CHOICE

There are times in our life when we must make choices. A choice is between good and evil, but one may choose a mixture of both. Many people choose a mixture which, in the sight of God, is no better than choosing evil. As Jesus said: *"So, because you are lukewarm, and neither hot nor cold, I will spit you out of my mouth." Revelation 3:16 (ESV)*

Therefore, good and evil are alternatives, and every human being must choose one alternative or the other. We are accountable for all our choices and for the actions that flow from them, regardless of the sin. Just as we are to choose, Adam, the first human being, also had to choose. He had to choose between believing and obeying God and disobeying Satan and disobeying God and obeying Satan. To obey is to believe in the person who gave you rules to follow; to disobey is to disbelieve the person who has given you rules to follow. Satan requires a person's permission to manipulate. He can get that permission from a person consciously or unconsciously. It can be given through a blood line and generational access or through individual access: *"Don't give the slanderous accuser, the Devil, an opportunity to manipulate you!" Ephesians 4:27 (TPT)*

Satan exploits the sins a person engages in. He focuses his strategies on the sin the person commits most frequently. For instance, if a person commits fornication more than he or she steals, Satan focuses his strategies and temptations on the fornication more than the stealing.

> To obey is to believe in the person who gave you rules to follow; to disobey is to disbelieve the person who has given you rules to follow.

The Spirit, the Soul, and the Body (Flesh)

A human being is composed of spirit, soul and body: *"Now may the God of peace himself sanctify you completely and may your whole spirit and soul and body be kept blameless at the coming of our Lord Jesus Christ." 1 Thessalonians 5:23 (ESV)*

Let us explore them individually:

1. **The Spirit:** The spirit component of the human being is the part that God communicates with. The human spirit is supposed to connect with the Spirit of God. This component is the part of us that houses the Holy Spirit and therefore could become born again. It cannot be

seen with the physical eye. *"The Spirit alone gives eternal life. Human effort accomplishes nothing. And the very words I have spoken to you are spirit and life." John 6:63 (NLT)*

2. **The Soul:** The soul is the seat of emotions (feelings), mind (thought), personality, will (decisions), and conscience. It is the component that mediates between the spirit and the flesh (body). It makes the decision to obey either the Spirit or the flesh. The soul decides to sin or be righteous. It is the soul that will face judgement and be allowed either to ascend to heaven or descend into hell. The soul (mind) can experience renewal and also cannot be seen with the physical organs of sight:

The soul that sinneth, it shall die. The son shall not bear the iniquity of the father, neither shall the father bear the iniquity of the son: the righteousness of the righteous shall be upon him, and the wickedness of the wicked shall be upon him. Ezekiel 18: 20 (KJV)

Do not be conformed to this world, but be transformed by the renewal of your mind, that by testing you may discern what is the will of God, what is good and acceptable and perfect. Romans 12:2 (ESV)

3. **The Flesh (Body):** The flesh or body is that part of a human being that can physically touch and be touched, see and been seen. It can find sin appealing, and inclines toward error. The five senses (sight, hearing,

taste, touch, and smell) are avenues of information for the organism that is the human body:

These three components—spirit, soul, and body work together and often tussle with one another. The flesh and the spirit are in a constant struggle for supremacy over the soul: *"For the desires of the flesh are against the Spirit, and the desires of the Spirit are against the flesh, for these are opposed to each other, to keep you from doing the things you want to do." Galatians. 5:17 (ESV)*

At the end of each tussle, the soul makes a decision. The spirit either surrenders to the flesh, or the flesh to the spirit. God expects our flesh to submit to the spirit, but Satan wants the spirit to submit to the flesh.

Let's see how these three components work and interact in the case of two different people.

Case 1: The Case of an Unrighteous Man

A man sees with his physical <u>eyes</u> a half-naked woman passing in front of his house. His soul processes what he sees. His mind, the <u>thought</u> component of his soul, begins to think lustfully of what he saw. The <u>emotion or feeling</u> component of his soul allows the sight of the naked woman to entice him. Throughout this process, his <u>conscience</u> tells him not to lust because it is sinful. His <u>will (his capacity to decide)</u> chooses to ignore his conscience. The next step involves the spirit component. His failure to obey his conscience indicates that his spirit is weak. So, he submits to the decision of his soul, thereby submitting to the flesh. By this submission the flesh is empowered and overcomes the soul and spirit. This fulfills Satan's desire.

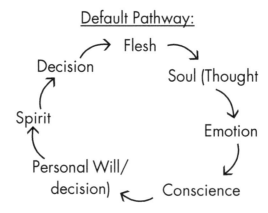

Default Pathway:

End Result of an Unrighteous man:
FLESH > SOUL > SPIRIT or SPIRIT< SOUL < FLESH

Case 2: The Case of a Righteous Man

A man sees with his physical eyes a half-naked woman passing in front of his house. At once his soul processes what he has seen. The thought (mind) begins to reason, indicating to him that although what he has seen is beautiful and pleasing to the eye, it can be a gateway to the sin of lust which is displeasing to God. The emotion (feeling) aspect of the soul remains intact and is fortified by the thought process. His conscience reinforces his conviction of how lust can offend God. His will chooses to obey his conscience due to his conviction and love for God. As soon as his spirit receives this information, it reports to the soul, strengthening it by acknowledging that such a decision to obey God's law is righteous. The soul then reports to the flesh, telling the eye to look away and resist potential temptation. It is the desire of God that your righteous will and spirit prevail over your flesh and not the other way around. *"This I say then, Walk in the Spirit, and ye shall not fulfil the lust of the flesh." Galatians 5:16 (KJV)*

The spirit was able to strengthen the decision of the soul because the spirit itself was strengthened. The spirit is strengthened through fasting, worship, praise, prayer, listening to spirit-filled Christian teachings, speaking in tongues, studying the Bible, discipline, and koinonia (communion or fellowship) with God.

Strengthening the spirit through discipline is extremely important. It is a form of mortifying the flesh and bringing it in subjection to the soul and spirit. Some of the means through which such discipline can occur were discussed in the solution sections of this book. Through this discipline, the soul is constantly renewed.

<u>Default Pathway:</u>

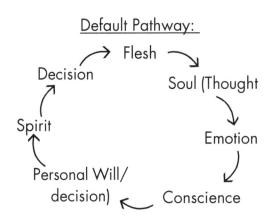

The End Result of the Righteous man:
SPIRIT> SOUL > FLESH or FLESH < SOUL < SPIRIT

Chapter 9:

THE FRUITFUL CHRISTIAN LIFESTYLE: GRACE AND REPENTANCE

THE FRUITFUL CHRISTIAN LIFESTYLE

A fruitful Christian lifestyle is sustained through the process of brokenness, daily consecration, perfect obedience, understanding the will of God, service, testing and conscious holiness.

1. Brokenness:
The first path towards living a fruitful Christian lifestyle is the process of brokenness. Brokenness entails admitting wrongs and surrendering to the sovereignty of God. Sometimes God has to allow His children to face challenging situations in order for them to attain brokenness. This can be demonstrated in Acts 9 where Saul who became Paul was blinded for three days as he approached Damascus to arrest the followers of Jesus. His blindness came from His encounter with Jesus Christ, but he regained his sight three days later. This encounter broke him, changed him, and renewed him. God delights in using people whom society tags as weak and feeble. But when He finds a man with strength, He breaks and

remolds them so they can see their weakness. To be a useful vessel of God, we must first allow the creator to break us like a clay pot and then remold us to fit the image of Christ Jesus.

2. Daily Consecration, Perfect Obedience and Understanding the Will of God

Consecration is the process of giving God permission to take total control over your life. It is a form of providing God license to destroy any satanic establishment in your life. The establishments that Satan manipulated and utilized become instruments God can use freely. God takes His time in demolishing and reconstructing these establishments, since it is a process that requires us to be carried along step by step. Consecration requires the surrender of our desires and will to God. At some point in our journey, our volitions will differ from God's. In fact, if we weigh our options, it might seem better to go with our own desire, but a consecrated man will subordinate his own will and align it with God's. Jesus set this example for us when he prayed in the garden of Gethsemane: *"My Father, if it be possible, let this cup pass from me; nevertheless, not as I will, but as you will"* Matthew 26:39 (ESV). This level of servanthood requires daily communion through prayer so your spirit is continually strengthened. Jesus also sets this example for us: *"Jesus left the upper room with his disciples and, as was his habit, went to the Mount of Olives, his place of secret prayer"* Luke 22:39 (TPT). If we faithfully practice daily consecration and perfect our obedience to the Holy Spirit, we will become trusted and reliable vessels of God. In fact, the Holy Spirit then becomes available to us and whispers Scriptures to our heart to assist us when we face ungodly sexual temptation, such as: *"I made a*

covenant with my eyes not to look lustfully at a young woman"
Job 31:1 (NIV)

> *Your personal will is not the only thing needing consecration. Your five senses, actions, flesh, opinion, thoughts, and whole self need it as well: I appeal to you therefore, brothers, by the mercies of God, to present your bodies as a living sacrifice, holy and acceptable to God, which is your spiritual worship. Do not be conformed to this world, but be transformed by the renewal of your mind, that by testing you may discern what is the will of God, what is good and acceptable and perfect. Romans 12:1-2 (ESV)*

3. Service:
After being saved by Jesus Christ, God calls us to service. Only those who accept God's call and meet His requirements are chosen. God chooses very few people as vessels for His purposes: *"For many are called, but few are chosen."* Matthew 22:14 (ESV)

> It is only reasonable to offer yourself as a vessel in bringing others to Christ Jesus so they, too, can be saved. Doing this is a great way to show gratitude to God for delivering us. Because of the great size of the harvest, God is constantly searching for laborers: *"The harvest is plentiful, but the workers are few"* Matthew 9:37 (NIV). Therefore, in order to accomplish a successful service in the vineyard of God, the Holy Spirit provides for us diverse gifts:

Each believer is given continuous revelation by the Holy Spirit to benefit not just himself but all. For example: The Spirit gives to one the gift of the word of wisdom. To another, the same Spirit gives the gift of the word of revelation knowledge. And to another, the same Spirit gives the gift of faith. And to another, the same Spirit gives gifts of healing. And to another the power to work miracles. And to another the gift of prophecy. And to another the gift to discern what the Spirit is speaking. And to another the gift of speaking different kinds of tongues. And to another the gift of interpretation of tongues. Remember, it is the same Holy Spirit who distributes, activates, and operates these different gifts as he chooses for each believer. 1 Corinthians 12:7-11 (TPT)

These gifts given to us by the Holy Spirit are for the body of Christ. In our service we must collaborate with one another, volunteering our time to spread and preach the Word of God as we travel, at our workplaces, on crusade grounds, on the streets, in the church, in the school, and everywhere else we can. Remember, we are the army of the Lord, and He depends on us to carry out our task as we depend on Him.

4. Testing and Continuous Holiness

Every Christian must pass through a period of testing. It is often through testing that our ranks in the spirit realm are increased. God never gives us more than we can carry, and He goes along with us in our journey. Just as God's faithful servant Job was tested, so are we going to be tested. A manufacturer of a product must test his product before releasing it for sale. If we can test our products, how much more God will who created us: *"For you, O God, have tested us; you have tried us as silver is tried."* Psalm. 66:10 (ESV)

Each test approved by God is never fruitless rather they produce steadfastness (James 1:2-4; see below). Each test can be passed or failed, and there are rewards for passing and consequences for failing. As we continue our journey, we are called to live a righteous life. Everything about our lives, from the way we talk to the way we dress and act, must preach the gospel of Jesus Christ. There is no room for hypocrisy; God detests it. We must therefore make holiness a lifestyle not only in our churches, but also outside them. You must get to the point where you see holiness, breathe holiness, hear holiness, speak holiness, feel holiness, think holiness, become one with and inseparable from holiness, until you become holiness itself because your heavenly father is holy: *"Follow peace with all men, and holiness, without which no man shall see the Lord"* Hebrew 12:14 (KJV)

Count it all joy, my brothers, when you meet trials of various kinds, for you know that the testing of your faith produces steadfastness. And let steadfastness have its full effect, that you may be perfect and complete, lacking in nothing. James 1:2-4 (ESV)

The Essence of Grace in Overcoming Sins of the Flesh

Grace is one of the things God provides His children. Once a demon is involved in the practice of a sexual sin, repentance would not be the only thing needed to secure deliverance. Repentance does not drive away the demons. Repentance only fulfills a part of the requirement for deliverance. Rather, it is the mercy and grace through the sacrificial death and glorious resurrection of Jesus Christ that delivers. All power lies in the Lord Jesus Christ, and it is His will that sin have no dominion over man for in Him lies all the grace we require: *For sin will have no dominion over you, since you are not under law but under grace. Romans 6:14 (ESV)*

It is the grace that Jesus provides that makes us uncomfortable and irritated by sexual sins after deliverance. It is that same grace that prevents us from going back to our sinful ways and assures us of the price we will receive at the end of our earthly journey.

Since we are already saved from the power of sin, we must align to the will and desire of God: *"He has saved us and called us to a holy life—not because of anything we have done but because of his own purpose and grace. This grace was given us in Christ Jesus before the beginning of time." 2 Timothy 1:9 (NIV)*

We do, however, have an assignment: the responsibility to guard our heart and mind with all diligence. They are the first territories assigned by God for us to protect. They are also the first treasures that Satan desires to steal from us. God provides you with the tools and weapons you need in order to carry out this assignment, but it is within your power to use them: *"Guard your heart above all else, for it determines the course of your life." Proverbs 4:23 (NLT)*

Christ Jesus has done the main work. He has paid the price of our iniquities and uncleanliness. We have been declared righteous and called to share in His righteousness as we repent from our sins. We must then believe in what we have received, trusting fully in the righteousness, mercy, and grace that Jesus provides us. Faith is the key to opening the gifts of God and peace is the reward of such faith.

> Faith is the key to opening the gifts of God and peace is the reward of such faith.

REPENT!

The day will come when everyone will stand before God and give an account for all he or she has done. No one will be able to claim ignorance of God's law. Those who undress a man or woman with their eyes will and take pleasure in masturbating will face judgement. Those who watch pornography will not escape that judgement. Those who engage in sexual immorality and fornication will also feel the wrath of God.

God's response to sexual immorality has remained constant: He detests it. This book has been written to help you. To let you know that there is a way out of all sexual sins. The help lies in the person of Jesus Christ. He saved me from all sexual immorality on the same day at the twinkling of an eye. He can save you too. You have to believe it. Pray with all of your heart to Him for help because the grace to abstain from sin lies within Him. Sometimes people remain in their sexual immoral urges and addictions because they do not believe they can ever be overcome. But once Jesus Christ delivers you, you will realize how much you genuinely hate sexual immorality.

For a long time, churches, pastors and churchgoers have trivialized the topic of sexual immorality. Its discussion has been limited and not dealt with thoroughly in many Christian gatherings. Meanwhile, this is the sin that drives many people to hell daily. It is a sin that Satan has used to keep people from going to heaven. This sin has held so many preachers of the gospel captive and limited their growth. Decide to deal with this issue today, and do not procrastinate! Tomorrow may be too late and may never come. If you were to interview those who have died, many of them would tell you about the plans they had for their tomorrow. Some will tell you they planned to repent the next day. But unfortunately, the next day never came for them. Rather, they encountered judgement and were sent to hell.

Who can withstand the judgement of God? Who can withstand His anger and wrath? There is no mercy after death, no forgiveness for those who have taken their last breath. Again, do not procrastinate when it comes to your salvation. Now is the moment. Not tomorrow, but now. Those who commit sexual immorality will be sent to hell and below is its description.

- Hell has worms that do not die–Mark 9:48
- Hell has fires that are not quenched–Mark 9:48
- There is smoke and no rest in hell – Revelation 14:11
- The soul is destroyed in hell – Matthew 10:28
- Hell is a fiery furnace, where they will experience great sorrow, pain, and anguish – Matthew 13:42
- Hell is a place of condemnation–John 5:28-30
- Hell is a place of eternal punishment – Matthew 25:46
- Hell is a place of eternal destruction, people there are banished from the Lord's presence and from the manifestation of His glorious power–2 Thessalonians 1:8-9
- Hell is a place of darkness, where there will be weeping and gnashing of teeth – Matthew 8:12
- The whole human body is thrown into hell – Matthew 5:29
- Hell has no water–Luke 16:23-25
- Hell is a place of unquenchable fire – Matthew 3:12
- Hell has a lake of fire and sulfur – Revelation 20:10
- People are tormented day and night forever and ever in hell – Revelation 20:10

There is nothing the Almighty does not know or see or hear. He even knows the secret thoughts, both the good and evil ones. He wants you to admit and speak your wrongs and then promise not to return to committing them. He knows your behavior before you try to alter it. So why not seek His mercy? He offers it to you today. Accept Him into your heart. He stands at the door of your heart knocking, waiting for you to answer and let Him in. He will deliver you and make you whiter than snow. You'll never regret your decision. I pray you shall not miss your salvation and deliverance. The Lord will cover you with His mercy and love, and at the last day

He will say to you, "Good and faithful servant, enter into the joy of your master." Amen.

> *{Hell is where} the worms that eat them do not die, and the fire is not quenched. Mark 9:48 (NIV)*

> *And the smoke of their severe suffering ascends into ages upon ages. Those who worship the wild beast and its image and receive the mark of its name will have no rest day or night." Revelation. 14:11 (TPT)*

> *Do not be afraid of those who kill the body but cannot kill the soul. Rather, be afraid of the One who can destroy both soul and body in hell. Matthew 10:28 (NIV)*

> *And they will throw them into the fiery furnace, where they will experience great sorrow, pain, and anguish. Matthew. 13:42 (TPT)*

> *So don't be amazed when I tell you these things, for there is a day coming when all who have ever died will hear my voice calling them back to life, and they will come out of their graves! Those who have done what is good will experience a resurrection to eternal life. And those who have practiced evil will taste the resurrection that brings them to condemnation! John 5:28-30 (TPT)*

> *Then they will go away to eternal punishment, but the righteous to eternal life. Matthew 25:46 (NIV)*

"...within a flame of fire. He will bring perfect and full justice to those who don't know God and on those who refuse to embrace the gospel of our Lord Jesus. They will suffer the penalty of eternal destruction, banished from the Lord's presence and from the manifestation of his glorious power. 2 Thessalonians 1:8-9 (TPT)

But the subjects of the kingdom will be thrown outside, into the darkness, where there will be weeping and gnashing of teeth." Matthew 8:12 (NIV)

If your right eye causes you to stumble, gouge it out and throw it away. It is better for you to lose one part of your body than for your whole body to be thrown into hell. Matthew 5:29 (NIV)

And being in torments in Hades, he lifted up his eyes and saw Abraham afar off, and Lazarus in his bosom. Then he cried and said, "Father Abraham, have mercy on me, and send Lazarus that he may dip the tip of his finger in water and cool my tongue; for I am tormented in this flame." But Abraham said, "Son, remember that in your lifetime you received your good things, and likewise Lazarus evil things; but now he is comforted and you are tormented." Luke 16:23-25 (NKJV)

His winnowing fork is in his hand, and he will clear his threshing floor, gathering his wheat into the barn and burning up the chaff with unquenchable fire. Matthew 3:12 (NIV)

Then the devil who had deceived them was thrown into the same place with the wild beast and the false prophet—the lake of fire and sulfur—where they will be tormented day and night forever and ever. Revelation 20:10 (TPT)

FOUR STEPS TO RECEIVING SALVATION

1. <u>Repentance towards God</u>

The first step to receiving salvation is repentance towards God. This step requires you to:

1. Admit and acknowledge your sin.
2. Voluntarily repent from your wicked and sinful ways.
3. Turn away from your sins to God and admit that it is He whom you have wronged.

4. Call out and confess your sins. This exposes to Jesus every hidden thing you have done in the past. Forsake all your sins and past ways, including sinful actions, thoughts, disobedience, words, self-righteousness, and omissions.

5. Renounce all involvements, affiliations, and help you have received from the satanic kingdom. Some examples are the occult, witch doctors, witchcraft, marine kingdom, and psychics. Ask Jesus to break every covenant you have made with Satan and his agents, directly or indirectly. Also, renounce any dedication and spirit that has claimed ownership of your soul. Renounce the flesh, its desires, and any promise Satan has offered you.

6. Ask Jesus for forgiveness and mercy.

These six points have been formulated into a salvation prayer.

Salvation Prayer

Lord Jesus Christ, I thank You for introducing Yourself to me through this book. Today I acknowledge my sins. I repent from my wicked and sinful ways. Today I turn away from my sins to You and I admit that it is You whom I have wronged. (Instruction → PAUSE: Verbally call out and confess your sins. In doing so, expose to Jesus Christ every hidden thing you have done in the past. Some of the sins you can repent from are your actions, thoughts, disobedience, words, self-righteousness, and omissions). **I forsake all my sins and sinful past ways. I renounce all involvements, affiliations and help I have received from the satanic kingdom.** (Some examples of affiliations and involvements with the satanic kingdom are the occult, witch doctors, witchcraft, marine kingdom, palm readers, and psychics). **Lord Jesus Christ, I ask you to break every covenant I have made directly and indirectly with Satan and his agents. I also renounce any dedication and spirit that has claimed ownership of my soul. I renounce the flesh, its desires and promises that Satan has offered me. Lord Jesus Christ, please be merciful unto me and forgive me as I accept you as my Lord and savior. I thank you for accepting me as your child and for saving me today. Amen.**

Congratulations! If you have said this salvation prayer, then by faith your name has transitioned from the Book of Death to the Book of Life. I would keep you in my prayers if you send me your name. You can reach me at elshaddai.feedback@gmail.com God bless you.

Scriptures on Repentance towards God:

> *"So let everyone in Israel know for certain that God has made this Jesus, whom you crucified, to be both Lord and Messiah!" Peter's words pierced their hearts, and they said to him and to the other apostles, "Brothers, what should we do?" Peter replied, "Each of you must <u>repent of your sins and turn to God</u>, and be <u>baptized in the name of Jesus Christ</u> for the forgiveness of your sins. Then you will <u>receive the gift of the Holy Spirit</u>." Acts 2:36-38 (NLT)*

> *Or do you despise the riches of His goodness, forbearance, and longsuffering, not knowing that*

the goodness of God leads you to <u>repentance</u>? Romans 2:4 (NKJV)

<u>Repent</u> therefore and be converted, that your sins may be blotted out, so that times of refreshing may come from the presence of the Lord Acts 3:19 (NKJV)

...how I kept back nothing that was helpful, but proclaimed it to you, and taught you publicly and from house to house, testifying to Jews, and also to Greeks, <u>repentance toward God</u> and <u>faith toward our Lord Jesus Christ.</u> Acts 20:20-21 (NKJV)

Then Jerusalem, all Judea, and all the region around the Jordan went out to him and were <u>baptized by him</u> in the Jordan, <u>confessing their sins</u>. Matthew 3:5-6 (NKJV)

He who covers his sins will not prosper, But whoever <u>confesses</u> and <u>forsakes them</u> will have mercy. Proverbs 28:13 (NKJV)

John came <u>baptizing</u> in the wilderness and preaching a baptism of <u>repentance for the remission of sins</u>. Then all the land of Judea, and those from Jerusalem, went out to him and were all baptized by him in the Jordan River, <u>confessing their sins.</u> Mark 1:4-5 (NKJV)

The Lord is not slack concerning His promise, as some count slackness, but is longsuffering toward *us, not willing that any should perish but that all should come to <u>repentance</u>. 2 Peter 3:9 (NKJV)*

2. <u>Faith in Jesus</u>

The second step to being saved involves doing the following:

- Profess your faith towards Jesus Christ with your mouth.
- Declare with your mouth that Jesus is Lord.
- Believe in your heart that God raised Jesus from the dead.
- Believe in the Lord Jesus Christ.
- Believe the Good News of His sacrificial death and glorious resurrection.

<u>Scriptures on Faith in Jesus</u>

...how I kept back nothing that was helpful, but proclaimed it to you, and taught you publicly and from house to house, testifying to Jews, and also to Greeks, <u>repentance toward God</u> and <u>faith toward our Lord Jesus Christ.</u> Acts 20:20-21 (NKJV)

<u>If you declare with your mouth, "Jesus is Lord,"</u> and <u>believe in your heart that God raised him from the dead,</u> you will be saved. For <u>it is with your heart</u>

that you believe and are justified, and it is with your mouth that you profess your faith and are saved. Romans 10:9-10 (NIV)

And he brought them out and said, "Sirs, what must I do to be saved?" So they said, "Believe on the Lord Jesus Christ, and you will be saved, you and your household." Acts 16:30-31 (NKJV)

Whoever believes the good news and is baptized will be saved, and whoever does not believe the good news will be condemned. Mark 16:16 (TPT)

3. Water Baptism

The third step to being saved is to be baptized with water. This has to be done in a Christian church. Water baptism tells the world that you now belong to Jesus Christ. It is a public confession to the world that you now identify as a follower of Jesus (that is, a Christian). Jesus said that if a man is not baptized, he cannot enter the kingdom of heaven.

Scriptures on Water Baptism

"So let everyone in Israel know for certain that God has made this Jesus, whom you crucified, to be both Lord and Messiah!" Peter's words pierced their hearts, and they said to him and to the other apostles, "Brothers, what should we do?" Peter replied, "Each of you must <u>repent of your sins and turn to God</u>, and be <u>baptized in the name of Jesus Christ</u> for the forgiveness of your sins. Then you will <u>receive the gift of the Holy Spirit.</u> Acts 2:36-38 (NLT)

There was a man of the Pharisees named Nicodemus, a ruler of the Jews. This man came to Jesus by night and said to Him, "Rabbi, we know that You are a teacher come from God; for no one can do these signs that You do unless God is with him." Jesus answered and said to him, "Most assuredly, I say to you, unless one is born again, he cannot see the kingdom of God." Nicodemus said to Him, "How can a man be born when he is old? Can he enter a second time into his mother's womb and be born?" Jesus answered, "Most assuredly, I say to you, unless one is born of <u>water and the Spirit,</u> he cannot enter the kingdom of God. John 3: 1-5 (NKJV)

Whoever <u>believes the good news</u> and is <u>baptized</u> will be <u>saved</u>, and whoever does not believe the good news will be condemned. Mark 16:16 (TPT)

...in which also he went and preached unto the spirits in prison, that aforetime were disobedient, when the longsuffering of God waited in the days of Noah, while the ark was a preparing, wherein few, that is, eight souls, were <u>saved</u> through water: which also after a true likeness doth now save you, even <u>baptism</u>, not the putting away of the filth of the flesh, but the interrogation of a good conscience toward God, through the resurrection of Jesus Christ. 1 Peter 3:19-21 (ASV)

4. <u>Holy Spirit Baptism</u>

Holy Spirit baptism is the final step to being saved. Once a person receives the baptism of the Holy Spirit, it becomes the intention of the Holy Spirit to invest His gifts in him or her. These gifts are diverse and given to each believer in order to edify the Church. A person can receive one or more of these spiritual gifts. There are nine of them listed in the *Book of 1 Corinthians* (12:7-11):

- The word of wisdom.
- The word of revealed knowledge.
- Faith.
- Healing.
- The power to work miracles.
- Prophecy.
- Discernment (of what the Spirit is speaking).
- Speaking different tongues.
- The interpretation of tongues.

These gifts are beneficial when utilized in a Christian gathering. Their importance has already been discussed in the sections on masturbation and solution to lust. But there are other important aspects. Speaking in tongues

- Allows one to know what prayer the Holy Spirit wants a person to pray
- Strengthens the spirit component of a person
- Deepens a person's intimacy with God
- Confuses Satan and his agents and throws them into a state of disarray, because they don't understand the language
- Helps a person know how the Holy Spirit wants them to pray
- Is weapon of spiritual warfare
- Allows a person to understand the deep mysteries of God
- Aids in fighting temptation
- Allows a person to know the will of God

- Transforms a Christian
- Strengthens a Christian's prayer life and energy
- Reveals divine secrets to men
- Permits people to hear the voice of God
- Aligns people to the will of God
- Allows the release of angels
- Energizes a person's prayer life
- Permits access to revelation
- Permits access to the expression of other spiritual gifts

A Prayer for Receiving the Baptism of the Holy Spirit

Instruction → Stretch forth your hands or raise them up as you say this prayer. Free yourself. Forget any issue or challenges you are facing and focus only on Jesus throughout the duration of this prayer.

Pray this prayer:

> Lord Jesus Christ, I thank you for sending the Holy Spirit to me. Holy Spirit come into my life at this moment. Break every barrier that can limit your flow into me. Let me have an upper-room experience at this moment. Fill me with your power, fire, and might. Fill me up until I overflow. Let the promise of Jesus be established in my life at this moment. Bless me with your gifts and anointing. Let there be an evidence of this outpouring through the gift of speaking in tongues. I thank you Holy Spirit for hearing my prayer.

Follow these instructions

- Breathe in, breathe out three times, asking the Holy Spirit to fill you as you pray.
- My prayer over you (stretch forth your hands): Holy Spirit, the third person of the Holy Trinity, I ask that you move like a mighty rushing wind into the life of your children. Release fire and power into them. Ask what you will, put on their lips the gift of speaking in tongues, and activate their prayer life in the name of Jesus Christ.
- Continue to pray until you are filled with the power of the Holy Spirit.
- Be sensitive at this moment and continue to engage in deep prayers. Open yourself to Him. You might experience a burning or electrocuting sensation on your body, or tears from your eyes or the shaking of hands and body or strange languages through your mouth or prophetic utterances or Holy Spirit chants. They are all evidence of the presence of the Holy Spirit. Continue to pray and ask to be completely filled. DO NOT DOUBT. If you open up to Him, He will fill you. Pray until you are filled. RECEIVE THE FIRE OF THE HOLYGHOST!

Scriptures on Holy Spirit Baptism

Now is the time for us to progress beyond the basic message of Christ and advance into perfection. The foundation has already been laid for us to build upon: turning away from our dead works to embrace <u>faith in God</u>, teaching about <u>different baptisms</u>, impartation by <u>the laying on of hands</u>, resurrection of the dead, and eternal judgment. So with God's enablement we will move on to deeper truths. Hebrews 6:1-3 (TPT)

"So let everyone in Israel know for certain that God has made this Jesus, whom you crucified, to be both Lord and Messiah!" Peter's words pierced their hearts, and they said to him and to the other apostles, "Brothers, what should we do?" Peter replied, "Each of you must repent of your sins and turn to God, and be baptized in the name of Jesus Christ for the forgiveness of your sins. Then you will receive the gift of the Holy Spirit." Acts 2:36-38 (NLT)

There was a man of the Pharisees named Nicodemus, a ruler of the Jews. This man came to Jesus by night and said to Him, "Rabbi, we know that You are a teacher come from God; for no one can do these signs that You do unless God is with him." Jesus answered and said to him, "Most assuredly, I say to you, unless one is born again, he cannot see the kingdom of God." Nicodemus said to Him, "How can a man be born when he is old? Can he enter a second time into his mother's womb and be born?" Jesus answered, "Most assuredly, I say to you, unless one is born of water and the Spirit, he cannot enter the kingdom of God. John 3: 1-5 (NKJV)

NOTE FROM TONYCLINTON

I am glad and thankful that you have read this life-changing book. I trust you have been blessed and transformed through it. Please feel free to share your personal stories, experiences, favorite principles and solutions from this book you found most helpful. I would be glad to hear from you. If you'd like to support the free distribution of this book in crusades, prayer meetings, educational institutions, evangelism, Christian fellowship, outreach, libraries, and other places at the author's discretion not mentioned, please email me: elshaddai.feedback@gmail.com

One great way you can spread this tool of illumination and deliverance to others is by word of mouth. Tell a friend about how helpful this book has been and consider leaving a review on the online store you bought it from. You can also send this book as a gift to loved ones, so they too can be transformed. For prayer requests, book distribution, seminars, conferences bookings and speaking engagements, again, email me at elshaddai.feedback@gmail.com

God bless you abundantly.

Appendix 1

PRAYER OF DEDICATION

Lord Jesus Christ, I thank You for introducing Yourself to me. I am a sinner and admit and acknowledge my sins and wicked ways. I repent from them and turn towards you today. I plead the blood of Jesus Christ as I ask for Your mercy and forgiveness. I break all ties, oaths, and covenants with the satanic kingdom whether they were made through my ancestral family or my own decision. I renounce all affiliations, involvements, powers, weapons, and aids I have received from the satanic kingdom. I also break all curses and spells that Satan has placed over me. I renounce Satan and all of his empty promises. I believe and accept that you, Jesus Christ, died for me on the cross of Calvary. I also believe in your glorious resurrection. Today I make you the Lord, savior, and master over my entire life. I give you access to all areas of my life as I am now a new creature in your kingdom of light. Break and remold me to conform me to your image. I enter into the merits of your sacrificial death and glorious resurrection. I thank you Lord Jesus Christ for hearing my prayers. Amen

PRAYER BEFORE DISCARDING SEXUAL OBJECTS USED FOR MASTURBATION

Lord Jesus Christ, I thank you for this illumination. I thank you for deciding to take away my addiction to sexual sin. Today, I acknowledge my wrongs and repent from all my sins. I plead the blood of Jesus Christ as I ask for your mercy and forgiveness. I freely break every link that connects me to these objects. I command the evil spirits associated with these to depart from my life in the name of Jesus Christ as I sprinkle this blessed oil and water on these items. Let the joy of salvation never depart from me as I do away with these items. I plead the blood of Jesus as defense against all accusations that Satan presents against me as a result of my past use of these items. I claim total restoration of my lost virtue, favor, and blessings in the name of Jesus Christ. I thank you Lord Jesus Christ for hearing my prayers. Amen.

PRAYER OF DELIVERANCE FROM MASTURBATION

A. Instruction
   - Discard all sexually immoral objects before proceeding to pray the prayers given below.

B. The Prayers:
   - Lord Jesus Christ I thank you for paying the price for my deliverance.
   - Lord Jesus Christ, I ask that you wash me clean of my iniquity through your precious blood and cleanse me from my sin.

- I ask that you blot out my transgressions and remove every record of sexual immorality that I have engaged in, in the name of Jesus Christ.
- I command every unclean spirit behind my addiction to masturbation to leave my life immediately in the name of Jesus Christ.
- I invoke the powers of the sacrificial death and glorious resurrection of Jesus Christ as I break every satanic covenant that I have made with Satan and his agents, directly or indirectly.
- I plead the blood of Jesus Christ to be my defense against every accusation that Satan and his agents continue to use against me to keep me in bondage, in the name of Jesus Christ.
- I command every unclean spirit to loosen their grip on my life, in the name of Jesus Christ.
- I terminate the influence of thrones and powers that have found expression in my life, in the name of Jesus Christ.
- I disconnect myself from every bodily fluid that has been taken and used in the kingdom of Satan to manipulate me, in the name of Jesus Christ.
- I shut down every route that has given Satan and unclean spirits access to life. I take back myself control as I am declared free from the addiction of masturbation, in the name of Jesus Christ.
- I command every stolen virtue, favor, and blessing to be restored in multiple folds, in the name of Jesus Christ.
- I thank you Lord Jesus Christ for hearing my prayers. Amen.

C. <u>Pray these scriptures with holy anger:</u>
- Psalm 51, Psalm 27, Psalm 68, Isaiah 40, Isaiah 61, Psalm 91, Psalm 23, Psalm 10:14

PRAYERS OF DELIVERANCE FROM PORNOGRAPHY

A. <u>Instruction</u>
- Delete all obscene material, sexually explicit pictures, audio, videos, notes, and recordings of others from your devices and discard all sexually immoral material and objects.

B. <u>Pray these prayers:</u>
- Lord Jesus Christ I thank you for paying the price for my deliverance.
- I ask, O Lord, that you forgive me for all the pornographic contents that I have consumed, in the name of Jesus Christ.
- I command every spirit responsible for my addiction to pornographic content to leave my life now, in the name of Jesus Christ.
- I command any deposit or residue of Satan in me to come out, in the name of Jesus Christ.
- I consecrate my eyes, ears, and mind to you, Jesus Christ.
- I plead the blood of Jesus as fortification against the accusations and proof that Satan and his agents present as reasons to keep me under bondage, in the name of Jesus Christ.

- I disconnect myself from my bodily fluid that has been held in the kingdom of Satan and used to make reference to me, in the name of Jesus Christ.
- I come against thrones and powers responsible for manipulating my life, in the name of Jesus Christ.
- I break every yoke, curse, and spell that Satan and his agent has placed on me that is responsible for my addiction to pornographic content, in the name of Jesus Christ.
- I recover in manifold ways everything Satan and his agents have taken from me, in the name of Jesus Christ.
- By the finished work of Christ, I command total restoration of all lost virtues, blessing, favor, connections, and gifts that Satan has stolen from me, in the name of Jesus Christ.
- I thank you Lord Jesus Christ for hearing my prayers. Amen.

C. Pray these scriptures with holy anger:
- Psalm 51, Psalm 27, Psalm 68, Isaiah 40, Isaiah 61, Psalm 91, Psalm 23, Psalm 10:14

PRAYER FOR DELIVERANCE FROM FORNICATION

A. Instructions
- Do not pursue further any sexually immoral relationship.
- Call out all the names of the people you had sexual immorality with that you can remember and ask Jesus for mercy. Also ask that every tie between you and them be broken in the name of Jesus Christ.

B. <u>Pray these prayers:</u>
- Lord Jesus Christ I thank you for paying the price for my deliverance.
- I ask, O Lord, that you forgive me for every form of sexual immorality I have engaged in, including fornication, in the name of Jesus Christ.
- By the death and resurrection of Jesus Christ, I command every evil and perverse spirit behind my addiction to fornication to leave my life now, in the name of Jesus Christ.
- I plead the blood of Jesus Christ as defense against every reason or evidence that Satan has presented against me, in the name of Jesus Christ.
- Let every curse and infirmity that has been laid on me as a result of my actions be removed, in the name of Jesus Christ.
- By the death and resurrection of Jesus Christ, I command every evil and perverse spirit behind my addiction to fornication to leave my life now, in the name of Jesus Christ.
- I command any of my bodily residue that is used to connect to me in the kingdom of Satan to disconnect, in the name of Jesus Christ.
- I command every perverse spirit to get out of my life and be disgraced, in the name of Jesus Christ.
- By the finished work of Jesus Christ on the cross, let there be restoration of my lost virtue, favor, and blessings, in the name of Jesus Christ.
- I thank you Lord Jesus Christ for hearing my prayers. Amen.

C. <u>Pray these scriptures with holy anger</u>
- Psalm 51, Psalm 27, Psalm 68, Isaiah 40, Isaiah 61, Psalm 91, Psalm 23, Psalm 10:14

PRAYER OF DELIVERANCE FROM LUST

A. <u>Pray these prayers:</u>
- Lord Jesus Christ I thank you for paying the price for my deliverance.
- I ask, O Lord, that you forgive me of all my sins in the name of Jesus Christ.
- By the death and resurrection of Jesus Christ, I command every evil spirit behind my addiction to lust to leave me, in the name of Jesus Christ.
- I plead the blood of Jesus Christ as my defense against the accusations of Satan and his agents, in the name of Jesus Christ.
- By the finished work of Jesus Christ on the cross of Calvary, I end every satanic manipulation of my mind from the satanic realm, in the name of Jesus Christ.
- In the name of Jesus Christ, I come against every lustful thought that Satan and his agents implanted in my mind.
- I dedicate my hands, feet, body, soul, spirit, five senses, and entire being as a vessel of God's service, in the name of Jesus Christ.
- Through the death and resurrection of Jesus Christ I shut down all satanic tools of manipulation through which Satan and his agents use in instilling lustful thoughts in me, in the name of Jesus Christ.

- I command every evil spirit responsible for my lust to evacuate from my life, in the name of Jesus Christ.
- I end every negative effect that my involvement in sexual immorality has made on my destiny, in the name of Jesus Christ.
- I ask you, Holy Spirit, to incubate me and fill my mind with godly thoughts, in the name of Jesus Christ.
- By the finished work of Jesus Christ, I command all my lost virtue, blessings, and favor to be restored in multiple folds, in the name of Jesus Christ.
- I thank you Lord Jesus Christ for hearing my prayers. Amen.

B. Pray these scriptures with holy anger
- Psalm 51, Psalm 27, Psalm 68, Isaiah 40, Isaiah 61, Psalm 91, Psalm 23, Psalm 10:14

PRAYER OF DELIVERANCE FROM MOMENTS OF EXTREME SEXUAL AROUSAL

Pray these prayers:

- Lord Jesus Christ I thank you for paying the price for my deliverance.
- Lord Jesus, I ask that you forgive me for allowing Satan and his agents access to my life.
- I command every spirit that causes me to experience moments of extreme sexual arousal to evacuate, in the name of Jesus Christ.

- I consecrate to God every faculty of mine that Satan and his agents use in making me experience moments of extreme sexual arousal, in the name of Jesus Christ.
- I terminate every manipulation in the satanic dark realm that manipulates me to experience moments of extreme sexual arousal, in the name of Jesus Christ.
- I declare an end to every experience of wet dreams, in the name of Jesus Christ.
- I plead the blood of Jesus Christ as my defense against every reason that Satan and his agents present to allow me to experience moments of extreme sexual arousal.
- I declare normalcy to all my hormones and sexual organs, in the name of Jesus Christ.
- By the finished work of Jesus Christ on the cross, let my destiny be released from the hands of the wicked, in the name of Jesus Christ.
- I declare normality and restoration in my life, in the name of Jesus Christ.
- I thank you, Lord Jesus Christ, for hearing my prayers. Amen.

Pray these scriptures with holy anger:

- Psalm 51, Psalm 27, Psalm 68, Isaiah 40, Isaiah 61, Psalm 91, Psalm 23, Psalm 10:14

PRAYER OF DELIVERANCE FROM SPIRIT SPOUSES

Instructions:

- Call out all the names that you can remember of people with whom you engaged in sexual immorality and ask Jesus for mercy. Also ask that every tie between you and them be broken in the name of Jesus Christ.

Pray the following prayers:

- Lord Jesus Christ I thank you for paying the price for my deliverance.
- Lord Jesus Christ, I ask that you blot out all my transgressions and shower your mercy upon my life, in the name of Jesus Christ.
- I renounce every conscious or unconscious marriage to spirit spouses, and I terminate the union, in the name of Jesus Christ.
- I break every generational curse that has exposed me to familiar spirits and spirit spouses, in the name of Jesus Christ.
- I invoke the power in the death and resurrection of Jesus Christ, and I ask that all wet-dream experiences in my life be ended, in the name of Jesus Christ.
- I disconnect myself from the activities of the satanic realm, in the name of Jesus Christ.
- I plead the blood of Jesus as I disconnect myself from every evil spirit spouse and spirit children that lay claim to me, in the name of Jesus Christ.
- I declare an end to eating in the dreams, in the name of Jesus Christ.

- I plead the blood of Jesus Christ as my defense against every accusation that Satan raises against me.
- I take all spirit spouses who have harassed me to the supreme court of heaven for judgement as I plead the blood of Jesus as my defense, in the name of Jesus Christ.
- I thank you, Lord Jesus Christ, for hearing my prayers. Amen.

Pray these scriptures with holy anger:

- Psalm 51, Psalm 38, Psalm 22, Psalm 27, Psalm 68, Isaiah 40, Isaiah 61, Psalm 91, Psalm 10, Psalm 23, Psalm 10:14

Appendix 2

PRAYER TO BLESS THE OIL

Lord God Almighty, creator of the universe and everything in it. I thank you for the gift of oil to humanity. I ask that you stretch forth your hand on this oil to bless it. Set this oil apart and make it your vessel. I now invoke the powers of the blessed Holy Trinity, God the Father, God the Son Jesus Christ, and God the Holy Spirit into this oil. Let it become consecrated, holy, and sanctified for your honor and glory, Lord.

Cause this oil to be an instrument of healing, blessing, and restoration. Let its users receive the merits that come through the anointing of the feet of Jesus, His sacrificial death, and glorious resurrection. May the power of Satan be ineffective wherever this oil is poured. Let this oil be a divine instrument to tear down satanic strongholds and break yokes, covenants, and affiliations with the satanic kingdom. May all demons be expelled, and their spells broken and removed from any item that this oil touches. Let those who use this oil be free from every infirmity, curse, and satanic manipulation. I thank you, Lord, for hearing my prayers. Amen

PRAYER TO BLESS THE WATER

Lord God Almighty, the creator of the universe. You made the waters on earth to refresh your creatures and I thank you.

I ask you to make this water a source of restoration, refreshment, and purification. I invoke the power of the blessed Holy Trinity, God the Father, God the Son Jesus Christ, and God the Holy Spirit into this water. Make it holy, consecrated, and sanctified. Let the Holy Spirit hover over the surface of this water as it did in the beginning. May this water be a source of deliverance like the water that came out of the side of Jesus Christ when He was pierced with a spear while hanging on the cross. May this water be a source of healing wherever it is sprinkled like the stirred pool of Bethesda. I pray that it become a source of blessing to whoever uses it. May your power in this water chase away Satan and his agents from any environment or object that this water touches. May your power in this water break down every stronghold, covenant, association, curse, spell, manipulation, and affiliation with the kingdom of Satan. And drive away all infirmities, sicknesses, and death from the body of those who drink it. I thank you, Lord, for hearing my prayers. Amen.

Appendix 3

BIBLE PASSAGES ON FORNICATION

- Or do you not know that your body is a temple of the Holy Spirit within you, whom you have from God? You are not your own. 1 Corinthians 6:19 (ESV)
- Do you not know that your bodies are members of Christ? Shall I then take the members of Christ and make them members of a prostitute? Never! Or do you not know that he who is joined to a prostitute becomes one body with her? For, as it is written, "The two will become one flesh." 1 Corinthians 6:15-16 (ESV)
- Do you not know that you are God's temple and that God's Spirit dwells in you? If anyone destroys God's temple, God will destroy him. For God's temple is holy, and you are that temple. 1 Corinthians 3:16-17 (ESV)
- How can a young man keep his way pure? By guarding it according to your word. With my whole heart I seek you; let me not wander from your commandments! Psalm 119:9-10 (ESV)
- Even as Sodom and Gomorrha, and the cities about them in like manner, giving themselves over to fornication, and going after strange flesh, are set forth for

an example, suffering the vengeance of eternal fire. Jude 1:7-8 (KJV)

- So God abandoned them to do whatever shameful things their hearts desired. As a result, they did vile and degrading things with each other's bodies. They traded the truth about God for a lie. So they worshiped and served the things God created instead of the Creator himself, who is worthy of eternal praise! Amen. That is why God abandoned them to their shameful desires. Even the women turned against the natural way to have sex and instead indulged in sex with each other. And the men, instead of having normal sexual relations with women, burned with lust for each other. Men did shameful things with other men, and as a result of this sin, they suffered within themselves the penalty they deserved. Romans 1:24-27 (NLT)

- Don't you realize that those who do wrong will not inherit the Kingdom of God? Don't fool yourselves. Those who indulge in sexual sin, or who worship idols, or commit adultery, or are male prostitutes, or practice homosexuality, or are thieves, or greedy people, or drunkards, or are abusive, or cheat people—none of these will inherit the Kingdom of God. 1 Corinthians 6:9-10 (NLT)

- Later, God condemned the cities of Sodom and Gomorrah and turned them into heaps of ashes. He made them an example of what will happen to ungodly people. But God also rescued Lot out of Sodom because he was a righteous man who was sick of the shameful immorality of the wicked people around him. Yes, Lot was a righteous man who was tormented in his soul by the wickedness he saw and heard day after day. So you see, the Lord knows how to rescue godly people from their trials, even while keeping the wicked under punishment until the day of final judgment. 2 Peter 2:6-9 (NLT)

- It is disgusting for a man to have sex with another man. Leviticus 18:22 (CEV)
- We know that the law is good when used correctly. For the law was not intended for people who do what is right. It is for people who are lawless and rebellious, who are ungodly and sinful, who consider nothing sacred and defile what is holy, who kill their father or mother or commit other murders. The law is for people who are sexually immoral, or who practice homosexuality, or are slave traders, liars, promise breakers, or who do anything else that contradicts the wholesome teaching. 1 Timothy 1:8-10 (NLT)

BIBLE PASSAGES ON MASTURBATION

- For this is the will of God, your sanctification: that you abstain from sexual immorality; that each one of you know how to control his own body in holiness and honor, not in the passion of lust like the Gentiles who do not know God. 1 Thessalonians 4:3-5 (ESV)
- Or do you not know that your body is a temple of the Holy Spirit within you, whom you have from God? You are not your own, for you were bought with a price. So glorify God in your body. 1 Corinthians 6:19–20 (ESV)
- But I say, walk by the Spirit, and you will not gratify the desires of the flesh. Galatians 5:16 (ESV)

- And if your right hand causes you to sin, cut it off and throw it away. For it is better that you lose one of your members than that your whole body go into hell. Matthew 5:30 (ESV)
- Since we have these promises, beloved, let us cleanse ourselves from every defilement of body and spirit, bringing holiness to completion in the fear of God. 2 Corinthians 7:1 (ESV)
- Beloved, I urge you as sojourners and exiles to abstain from the passions of the flesh, which wage war against your soul. 1 Peter 2:11 (ESV)

BIBLE PASSAGES ON PORNOGRAPHY

- I have made a covenant with my eyes; how then could I gaze at a virgin? Job 31:1 (ESV)
- Turn my eyes from looking at worthless things; and give me life in your ways. Psalm 119:37 (ESV)
- I will not set before my eyes anything that is worthless. I hate the work of those who fall away; it shall not cling to me. Psalm 101:3 (ESV)
- It happened, late one afternoon, when David arose from his couch and was walking on the roof of the king's house, that he saw from the roof a woman bathing; and the woman was very beautiful. And David sent and inquired about the woman. And one said, "Is not this Bathsheba, the daughter of Eliam, the wife of Uriah the Hittite?" So David sent messengers and took her, and she came to him, and he lay with her. (Now she had been purifying herself from her uncleanness.) Then she returned to her house. And

the woman conceived, and she sent and told David, "I am pregnant." 2 Samuel 11:2-5 (ESV)

- "You have heard that it was said, 'You shall not commit adultery.' But I say to you that everyone who looks at a woman with lustful intent has already committed adultery with her in his heart. Matthew 5:27-28 (ESV)
- But each person is tempted when he is lured and enticed by his own desire. Then desire when it has conceived gives birth to sin, and sin when it is fully grown brings forth death. James 1:14-15 (ESV)
- For all that is in the world—the desires of the flesh and the desires of the eyes and pride of life—is not from the Father but is from the world. 1 John 2:16 (ESV)

BIBLE PASSAGES ON LUST AND EXTREME SEXUAL AROUSAL

- Your eyes will see strange sights, and your mind will imagine confusing things. Proverbs 23:33 (NIV)
- But I say to you that everyone who looks at a woman with lustful intent has already committed adultery with her in his heart. Matthew 5:28 (ESV)
- I have made a covenant with my eyes; how then could I gaze at a virgin? Job 31:1 (ESV)
- For the time that is past suffices for doing what the Gentiles want to do, living in sensuality, passions, drunkenness, orgies, drinking parties, and lawless idolatry. 1 Peter 4:3 (ESV)
- Do not desire her beauty in your heart, and do not let her capture you with her eyelashes. Proverbs 6:25 (ESV)

- Beloved, I urge you as sojourners and exiles to abstain from the passions of the flesh, which wage war against your soul. 1 Peter 2:11 (ESV)
- Put to death therefore what is earthly in you: sexual immorality, impurity, passion, evil desire, and covetousness, which is idolatry. Colossians 3:5 (ESV)
- For this is the will of God, your sanctification: that you abstain from sexual immorality; that each one of you know how to control his own body in holiness and honor, not in the passion of lust like the Gentiles who do not know God; that no one transgress and wrong his brother in this matter, because the Lord is an avenger in all these things, as we told you beforehand and solemnly warned you. For God has not called us for impurity, but in holiness. 1 Thessalonians 4:3-8 (ESV)
- Therefore, God gave them up in the lusts of their hearts to impurity, to the dishonoring of their bodies among themselves, because they exchanged the truth about God for a lie and worshiped and served the creature rather than the Creator, who is blessed forever! Amen. For this reason, God gave them up to dishonorable passions. For their women exchanged natural relations for those that are contrary to nature; and the men likewise gave up natural relations with women and were consumed with passion for one another, men committing shameless acts with men and receiving in themselves the due penalty for their error. Romans 1:24-27 (ESV)
- For all that is in the world—the desires of the flesh and the desires of the eyes and pride in possessions—is

not from the Father but is from the world. 1 John 2:16 (ESV)

- Blessed is the man who remains steadfast under trial, for when he has stood the test he will receive the crown of life, which God has promised to those who love him. Let no one say when he is tempted, "I am being tempted by God," for God cannot be tempted with evil, and he himself tempts no one. But each person is tempted when he is lured and enticed by his own desire. Then desire when it has conceived gives birth to sin, and sin when it is fully grown brings forth death. James 1:12-15 (ESV)
- So flee youthful passions and pursue righteousness, faith, love, and peace, along with those who call on the Lord from a pure heart. 2 Timothy 2:22 (ESV)
- And those who belong to Christ Jesus have crucified the flesh with its passions and desires. Galatians 5:24 (ESV)
- Among whom we all once lived in the passions of our flesh, carrying out the desires of the body and the mind, and were by nature children of wrath, like the rest of mankind. Ephesians 2:3 (ESV)

BIBLE PASSAGES ON SEXUAL IMMORALITY

- Flee from sexual immorality. Every other sin a person commits is outside the body, but the sexually immoral person sins against his own body. Or do you not know that your body is a temple of the Holy Spirit within you, whom you have from God? You are not your own, for you were bought with a price. So glorify God in your body. 1 Corinthians 6:18-20 (ESV)

- But sexual immorality and all impurity or covetousness must not even be named among you, as is proper among saints. Ephesians 5:3 (ESV)
- Now the works of the flesh are evident: sexual immorality, impurity, sensuality, idolatry, sorcery, enmity, strife, jealousy, fits of anger, rivalries, dissensions, divisions, envy, drunkenness, orgies, and things like these. I warn you, as I warned you before, that those who do such things will not inherit the kingdom of God. But the fruit of the Spirit is love, joy, peace, patience, kindness, goodness, faithfulness, gentleness, self-control; against such things there is no law. And those who belong to Christ Jesus have crucified the flesh with its passions and desires. Galatians 5:19-24 (ESV)
- With much seductive speech she persuades him; with her smooth talk she compels him. All at once he follows her, as an ox goes to the slaughter, or as a stag is caught fast till an arrow pierces its liver; as a bird rushes into a snare; he does not know that it will cost him his life. And now, O sons, listen to me, and be attentive to the words of my mouth. Let not your heart turn aside to her ways; do not stray into her paths, for many a victim has she laid low, and all her slain are a mighty throng. Her house is the way to Sheol, going down to the chambers of death. Proverbs 7:21-27 (ESV)
- Put to death therefore what is earthly in you: sexual immorality, impurity, passion, evil desire, and covetousness, which is idolatry. Colossians 3:5 (ESV)

- With whom the kings of the earth have committed sexual immorality, and with the wine of whose sexual immorality the dwellers on earth have become drunk. Revelation 17:2 (ESV)
- But as for the Gentiles who have believed, we have sent a letter with our judgment that they should abstain from what has been sacrificed to idols, and from blood, and from what has been strangled, and from sexual immorality. Acts 21:25 (ESV)
- For all nations have drunk the wine of the passion of her sexual immorality, and the kings of the earth have committed immorality with her, and the merchants of the earth have grown rich from the power of her luxurious living. Revelations 18:3 (ESV)
- "You are doing the works your father did." They said to him, "We were not born of sexual immorality. We have one Father—even God." John 8:41 (ESV)
- The woman was arrayed in purple and scarlet, and adorned with gold and jewels and pearls, holding in her hand a golden cup full of abominations and the impurities of her sexual immorality. Revelation 17:4 (ESV)
- Finally, then, brothers, we ask and urge you in the Lord Jesus, that as you received from us how you ought to walk and to please God, just as you are doing, that you do so more and more. For you know what instructions we gave you through the Lord Jesus. For this is the will of God, your sanctification: that you abstain from sexual immorality; that each one of you know how to control his own body in holiness and honor, not in the passion of lust like the Gentiles who do not know God. 1 Thessalonians 4:1-5 (ESV)

- For this is the will of God, your sanctification: that you abstain from sexual immorality; that each one of you know how to control his own body in holiness and honor, not in the passion of lust like the Gentiles who do not know God; that no one transgress and wrong his brother in this matter, because the Lord is an avenger in all these things, as we told you beforehand and solemnly warned you. For God has not called us for impurity, but in holiness. 1 Thessalonians 4:3-7 (ESV)
- But I have this against you, that you tolerate that woman Jezebel, who calls herself a prophetess and is teaching and seducing my servants to practice sexual immorality and to eat food sacrificed to idols. Revelation 2:20 (ESV)
- But I have a few things against you: you have some there who hold the teaching of Balaam, who taught Balak to put a stumbling block before the sons of Israel, so that they might eat food sacrificed to idols and practice sexual immorality. Revelation 2:14 (ESV)
- For out of the heart come evil thoughts, murder, adultery, sexual immorality, theft, false witness, slander. Matthew 15:19 (ESV)
- I wrote to you in my letter not to associate with sexually immoral people— not at all meaning the sexually immoral of this world, or the greedy and swindlers, or idolaters, since then you would need to go out of the world. But now I am writing to you not to associate with anyone who bears the name of brother if he is guilty of sexual immorality or greed, or is an idolater, reviler, drunkard, or swindler—not even to eat with such a one. 1 Corinthians 5:9-11 (ESV)

- But sexual immorality and all impurity or covetousness must not even be named among you, as is proper among saints. Let there be no filthiness nor foolish talk nor crude joking, which are out of place, but instead let there be thanksgiving. For you may be sure of this, that everyone who is sexually immoral or impure, or who is covetous (that is, an idolater), has no inheritance in the kingdom of Christ and God. Ephesians 5:3-5 (ESV)
- But should write to them to abstain from the things polluted by idols, and from sexual immorality, and from what has been strangled, and from blood. Acts 15:20 (ESV)
- That you abstain from what has been sacrificed to idols, and from blood, and from what has been strangled, and from sexual immorality. If you keep yourselves from these, you will do well. Farewell. Acts 15:29 (ESV)
- But because of the temptation to sexual immorality, each man should have his own wife and each woman her own husband. 1 Corinthians 7:2 (ESV)
- Put to death therefore what is earthly in you: sexual immorality, impurity, passion, evil desire, and covetousness, which is idolatry. Colossians 3:5 (ESV)
- For you may be sure of this, that everyone who is sexually immoral or impure, or who is covetous (that is, an idolater), has no inheritance in the kingdom of Christ and God. Ephesians. 5:5 (ESV)
- For this is the will of God, your sanctification: that you abstain from sexual immorality. 1 Thessalonians 4:3 (ESV)

- We must not indulge in sexual immorality as some of them did, and twenty-three thousand fell in a single day. 1 Corinthians 10:8 (ESV)
- But as for the cowardly, the faithless, the detestable, as for murderers, the sexually immoral, sorcerers, idolaters, and all liars, their portion will be in the lake that burns with fire and sulfur, which is the second death. Revelation 21:8 (ESV)
- Food is meant for the stomach and the stomach for food"—and God will destroy both one and the other. The body is not meant for sexual immorality, but for the Lord, and the Lord for the body. And God raised the Lord and will also raise us up by his power. Do you not know that your bodies are members of Christ? Shall I then take the members of Christ and make them members of a prostitute? Never! Or do you not know that he who is joined to a prostitute becomes one body with her? For, as it is written, "The two will become one flesh." But he who is joined to the Lord becomes one spirit with him. 1 Corinthians 6:13-17 (ESV)
- It is actually reported that there is sexual immorality among you, and of a kind that is not tolerated even among pagans, for a man has his father's wife. 1 Corinthians 5:1 (ESV)
- Just as Sodom and Gomorrah and the surrounding cities, which likewise indulged in sexual immorality and pursued unnatural desire, serve as an example by undergoing a punishment of eternal fire. Jude 1:7 (ESV)
- I fear that when I come again my God may humble me before you, and I may have to mourn over many of those who sinned earlier and have not repented

of the impurity, sexual immorality, and sensuality that they have practiced. 2 Corinthians 12:21 (ESV)

- And he said, "What comes out of a person is what defiles him. For from within, out of the heart of man, come evil thoughts, sexual immorality, theft, murder, adultery, coveting, wickedness, deceit, sensuality, envy, slander, pride, foolishness. All these evil things come from within, and they defile a person." Mark 7:20-23 (ESV)
- That no one is sexually immoral or unholy like Esau, who sold his birthright for a single meal. Hebrew 12:16 (ESV)
- Outside are the dogs and sorcerers and the sexually immoral and murderers and idolaters, and everyone who loves and practices falsehood. Revelation 22:15 (ESV)
- For out of the heart come evil thoughts, murder, adultery, sexual immorality, theft, false witness, slander. These are what defile a person. But to eat with unwashed hands does not defile anyone. Matthew 15:19-20 (ESV)
- I gave her time to repent, but she refuses to repent of her sexual immorality. Revelation 2:21 (ESV)
- And the kings of the earth, who committed sexual immorality and lived in luxury with her, will weep and wail over her when they see the smoke of her burning. Revelation 18:9 (ESV)
- And you shall not lie sexually with your neighbor's wife and so make yourself unclean with her. Leviticus 18:20 (ESV)
- "Cursed be anyone who lies with his father's wife, because he has uncovered his father's nakedness."

And all the people shall say, "Amen." "Cursed be anyone who lies with any kind of animal." And all the people shall say, "Amen." "Cursed be anyone who lies with his sister, whether the daughter of his father or the daughter of his mother." And all the people shall say, "Amen." "Cursed be anyone who lies with his mother-in-law." And all the people shall say, "Amen." Deuteronomy 27:20-23 (ESV)

- "And to the angel of the church in Thyatira write: 'The words of the Son of God, who has eyes like a flame of fire, and whose feet are like burnished bronze. I know your works, your love and faith and service and patient endurance, and that your latter works exceed the first. But I have this against you, that you tolerate that woman Jezebel, who calls herself a prophetess and is teaching and seducing my servants to practice sexual immorality and to eat food sacrificed to idols. I gave her time to repent, but she refuses to repent of her sexual immorality. Behold, I will throw her onto a sickbed, and those who commit adultery with her I will throw into great tribulation, unless they repent of her works, and I will strike her children dead. And all the churches will know that I am he who searches mind and heart, and I will give to each of you according to your works." Revelation 2:18-23 (ESV)

- You shall not uncover the nakedness of your father's wife's daughter, brought up in your father's family, since she is your sister. You shall not uncover the nakedness of your father's sister; she is your father's relative. You shall not uncover the nakedness of your mother's sister, for she is your mother's relative. You shall not uncover the nakedness of your father's brother, that is, you shall not approach his wife; she is your aunt. You shall not uncover the nakedness of your daughter-in-law; she is your son's wife, you shall not uncover her nakedness. You shall not uncover the nakedness of your brother's wife; it is your brother's nakedness. You shall not uncover the nakedness of a woman and of her daughter, and you shall not take her son's daughter or her daughter's daughter to uncover her nakedness; they are relatives; it is depravity. And you shall not take a woman as a rival wife to her sister, uncovering her nakedness while her sister is still alive. Leviticus 18:11-18 (ESV)

- Understanding this, that the law is not laid down for the just but for the lawless and disobedient, for the ungodly and sinners, for the unholy and profane, for those who strike their fathers and mothers, for murderers, the sexually immoral, men who practice homosexuality, enslavers, liars, perjurers, and whatever else is contrary to sound doctrine. 1 Timothy 1:9-10 (ESV)

- If a man lies with a male as with a woman, both of them have committed an abomination; they shall surely be put to death; their blood is upon them. Leviticus 20:13 (ESV)

- You shall not lie with a male as with a woman; it is an abomination. Leviticus 18:22 (ESV)

- Nor did they repent of their murders or their sorceries or their sexual immorality or their thefts. Revelation 9:21 (ESV)

- If a man commits adultery with another man's wife—with the wife of his neighbor—both the adulterer and the adulteress are to be put to death. If a man has sexual relations with his father's wife, he has dishonored his father. Both the man and the woman are to be put to death; their blood will be on their own heads. If a man has sexual relations with his daughter-in-law, both of them are to be put to death. What they have done is a perversion; their blood will be on their own heads. If a man has sexual relations with a man as one does with a woman, both of them have done what is detestable. They are to be put to death; their blood will be on their own heads. If a man marries both a woman and her mother, it is wicked. Both he and they must be burned in the fire, so that no wickedness will be among you. If a man has sexual relations with an animal, he is to be put to death, and you must kill the animal. If a woman approaches an animal to have sexual relations with it, kill both the woman and the animal. They are to be put to death; their blood will be on their own heads. Leviticus 20:10-16 (NIV)

- Just as Sodom and Gomorrah and the surrounding cities, which likewise indulged in sexual immorality and pursued unnatural desire, serve as an example by undergoing a punishment of eternal fire. Jude 1:7 (ESV)
- But sexual immorality and all impurity or covetousness must not even be named among you, as is proper among saints. Ephesians 5:3 (ESV)
- For this reason, God gave them up to dishonorable passions. For their women exchanged natural relations for those that are contrary to nature; and the men likewise gave up natural relations with women and were consumed with passion for one another, men committing shameless acts with men and receiving

in themselves the due penalty for their error. Romans 1:26-27 (ESV)

- The sexually immoral, men who practice homosexuality, enslavers, liars, perjurers, and whatever else is contrary to sound doctrine. 1 Timothy 1:10 (ESV)

BIBLE PASSAGES ON ADULTERY

- He who commits adultery lacks sense; he who does it destroys himself. Proverbs 6:32 (ESV)
- You shall not commit adultery. Exodus. 20:14 (ESV)
- Let marriage be held in honor among all, and let the marriage bed be undefiled, for God will judge the sexually immoral and adulterous. Hebrews 13:4 (ESV)
- They have eyes full of adultery, insatiable for sin. They entice unsteady souls. They have hearts trained in greed. Accursed children! Forsaking the right way, they have gone astray. They have followed the way of Balaam, the son of Beor, who loved gain from wrongdoing, but was rebuked for his own transgression; a speechless donkey spoke with human voice and restrained the prophet's madness. These are waterless springs and mists driven by a storm. For them the gloom of utter darkness has been reserved. For, speaking loud boasts of folly, they entice by sensual passions of the flesh those who are barely escaping from those who live in error. 2 Peter 2:14-18 (ESV)
- He who commits adultery lacks sense; he who does it destroys himself. He will get wounds and dishonor, and his disgrace will not be wiped away. Proverbs 6:32-33 (ESV)

- If a man commits adultery with the wife of his neighbor, both the adulterer and the adulteress shall surely be put to death. Leviticus 20:10 (ESV)
- If a man is discovered committing adultery, both he and the woman must die. In this way, you will purge Israel of such evil. Deuteronomy. 22:22 (NLT)
- Everyone who divorces his wife and marries another commits adultery, and he who marries a woman divorced from her husband commits adultery. Luke 16:18 (ESV)
- Let marriage be held in honor among all, and let the marriage bed be undefiled, for God will judge the sexually immoral and adulterous. Hebrews 13:4 (ESV)
- Or do you not know that the unrighteous will not inherit the kingdom of God? Do not be deceived: neither the sexually immoral, nor idolaters, nor adulterers, nor men who practice homosexuality, nor thieves, nor the greedy, nor drunkards, nor revilers, nor swindlers will inherit the kingdom of God. 1 Corinthians 6:9-10 (ESV)
- But I say to you that everyone who divorces his wife, except on the ground of sexual immorality, makes her commit adultery, and whoever marries a divorced woman commits adultery. Matthew 5:32 (ESV)
- And he said to them, "Whoever divorces his wife and marries another commits adultery against her, and if she divorces her husband and marries another, she commits adultery." Mark 10:11-12 (ESV)
- And I say to you: whoever divorces his wife, except for sexual immorality, and marries another, commits adultery." Matthew 19:9 (ESV)

- You have heard that it was said, "You shall not commit adultery." But I say to you that everyone who looks at a woman with lustful intent has already committed adultery with her in his heart. Matthew 5:27-28 (ESV)
- My son, be attentive to my wisdom; incline your ear to my understanding, that you may keep discretion, and your lips may guard knowledge. For the lips of a forbidden woman drip honey, and her speech is smoother than oil, but in the end she is bitter as worm-wood, sharp as a two-edged sword. Her feet go down to death; her steps follow the path to Sheol. Proverbs 5:1-6 (ESV)
- My son, keep my words and treasure up my com-mandments with you; keep my commandments and live; keep my teaching as the apple of your eye; bind them on your fingers; write them on the tablet of your heart. Say to wisdom, "You are my sister," and call insight your intimate friend, to keep you from the for-bidden woman, from the adulteress with her smooth words. Proverbs 7:1-5 (ESV)
- So you will be delivered from the forbidden woman, from the adulteress with her smooth words, who for-sakes the companion of her youth and forgets the covenant of her God; for her house sinks down to death, and her paths to the departed; none who go to her come back, nor do they regain the paths of life. Proverbs 2:16-19 (ESV)
- But in the prophets of Jerusalem I have seen a hor-rible thing: they commit adultery and walk in lies; they strengthen the hands of evildoers, so that no one turns from his evil; all of them have become like Sodom

to me, and its inhabitants like Gomorrah. Jeremiah 23:14 (ESV)
- Can a man carry fire next to his chest and his clothes not be burned? Or can one walk on hot coals and his feet not be scorched? So is he who goes in to his neighbor's wife; none who touches her will go unpunished. Proverbs 6:27-29 (ESV)
- If a man is found lying with the wife of another man, both of them shall die, the man who lay with the woman, and the woman. So you shall purge the evil from Israel. Deuteronomy 22:22 (ESV)
- She saw that for all the adulteries of that faithless one, Israel, I had sent her away with a decree of divorce. Yet her treacherous sister Judah did not fear, but she too went and played the whore. Jeremiah 3:8 (ESV)
- The scribes and the Pharisees brought a woman who had been caught in adultery, and placing her in the midst. John 8:3 (ESV)
- Let marriage be held in honor among all, and let the marriage bed be undefiled, for God will judge the sexually immoral and adulterous. Hebrews 13:4 (ESV)

BIBLE PASSAGES ON PROSTITUTION

- Or do you not know that he who is joined to a prostitute becomes one body with her? For, as it is written, "The two will become one flesh. 1 Corinthians 6:16 (ESV)
- For the price of a prostitute is only a loaf of bread, but a married woman hunts down a precious life. Proverbs 6:26 (ESV)

- None of the daughters of Israel shall be a cult prostitute, and none of the sons of Israel shall be a cult prostitute. You shall not bring the fee of a prostitute or the wages of a dog into the house of the Lord your God in payment for any vow, for both of these are an abomination to the Lord your God. Deuteronomy 23:17-18 (ESV)

- Do you not know that your bodies are members of Christ? Shall I then take the members of Christ and make them members of a prostitute? Never! Or do you not know that he who is joined to a prostitute becomes one body with her? For, as it is written, "The two will become one flesh." But he who is joined to the Lord becomes one spirit with him. Flee from sexual immorality. Every other sin a person commits is outside the body, but the sexually immoral person sins against his own body. Or do you not know that your body is a temple of the Holy Spirit within you, whom you have from God? You are not your own. 1 Corinthians 6:15-20 (ESV)

- You also played the whore with the Egyptians, your lustful neighbors, multiplying your whoring, to provoke me to anger. Ezekiel 16:26 (ESV)

- For his judgments are true and just; for he has judged the great prostitute who corrupted the earth with her immorality, and has avenged on her the blood of his servants. Revelation 19:2 (ESV)

- None of the daughters of Israel shall be a cult prostitute, and none of the sons of Israel shall be a cult prostitute. You shall not bring the fee of a prostitute or the wages of a dog into the house of the Lord your God in payment for any vow, for both of these are an abomination to the Lord your God. Deuteronomy 23:17-18 (ESV)

- And from the land he exterminated the remnant of the male cult prostitutes who remained in the days of his father Asa. 1 Kings 22:46 (ESV)
- And there were also male cult prostitutes in the land. They did according to all the abominations of the nations that the Lord drove out before the people of Israel. 1 Kings 14:24 (ESV)
- To preserve you from the evil woman, from the smooth tongue of the adulteress. Do not desire her beauty in your heart, and do not let her capture you with her eyelashes; for the price of a prostitute is only a loaf of bread, but a married woman hunts down a precious life. Proverbs 6:24-26 (ESV)
- A widow, or a divorced woman, or a woman who has been defiled, or a prostitute, these he shall not marry. But he shall take as his wife a virgin of his own people. Leviticus 21:14 (ESV)
- And he broke down the houses of the male cult prostitutes who were in the house of the Lord, where the women wove hangings for the Asherah. 2 Kings 23:7 (ESV)
- You engaged in prostitution with the Assyrians too, because you were insatiable; and even after that, you still were not satisfied. Then you increased your promiscuity to include Babylonia, a land of merchants, but even with this you were not satisfied. I am filled with fury against you, declares the Sovereign Lord, when you do all these things, acting like a brazen prostitute! When you built your mounds at every street corner and made your lofty shrines in every public square,

you were unlike a prostitute, because you scorned payment. You adulterous wife! You prefer strangers to your own husband! All prostitutes receive gifts, but you give gifts to all your lovers, bribing them to come to you from everywhere for your illicit favors. So, in your prostitution you are the opposite of others; no one runs after you for your favors. You are the very opposite, for you give payment and none is given to you. Therefore, you prostitute, hear the word of the Lord! This is what the Sovereign Lord says: Because you poured out your lust and exposed your naked body in your promiscuity with your lovers, and because of all your detestable idols, and because you gave them your children's blood, therefore I am going to gather all your lovers, with whom you found pleasure, those you loved as well as those you hated. I will gather them against you from all around and will strip you in front of them, and they will see you stark naked. I will sentence you to the punishment of women who commit adultery and who shed blood; I will bring on you the blood vengeance of my wrath and jealous anger. Then I will deliver you into the hands of your lovers, and they will tear down your mounds and destroy your lofty shrines. They will strip you of your clothes and take your fine jewelry and leave you stark naked. They will bring a mob against you, who will stone you and hack you to pieces with their swords. They will burn down your houses and inflict punishment on you in the sight of many women. I will put a stop to your prostitution, and you will no longer pay your lovers. Then my wrath against you will subside and my jealous anger will turn away from you; I will be calm and no longer angry. Ezekiel 16: 28-42 (NIV)

- Do not profane your daughter by making her a prostitute, lest the land fall into prostitution and the land become full of depravity. Leviticus 19:29 (ESV)

- For at the window of my house I have looked out through my lattice, and I have seen among the simple, I have perceived among the youths, a young man lacking sense, passing along the street near her corner, taking the road to her house in the twilight, in the evening, at the time of night and darkness. And behold, the woman meets him, dressed as a prostitute, wily of heart. She is loud and wayward; her feet do not stay at home; now in the street, now in the market, and at every corner she lies in wait. She seizes him and kisses him, and with bold face she says to him, "I had to offer sacrifices, and today I have paid my vows; so now I have come out to meet you, to seek you eagerly, and I have found you. I have spread my couch with coverings, colored linens from Egyptian linen; I have perfumed my bed with myrrh, aloes, and cinnamon. Come, let us take our fill of love till morning; let us delight ourselves with love. For my husband is not at home; he has gone on a long journey; he took a bag of money with him; at full moon he will come home." With much seductive speech she persuades him; with her smooth talk she compels him. All at once he follows her, as an ox goes to the slaughter, or as a stag is caught fast till an arrow pierces its liver; as a bird rushes into a snare; he does not know that it will cost him his life. And now, O sons, listen to me, and be attentive to the words of my mouth. Let not your heart turn aside to her ways; do not stray into her paths, for many a victim has she laid low, and all her slain are a mighty throng. Her house is the way to Sheol, going down to the chambers of death. Proverbs 7: 6-27 (ESV)

- And the daughter of any priest, if she profanes herself by whoring, profanes her father; she shall be burned with fire. Leviticus 21:9 (ESV)

- Then one of the seven angels who had the seven bowls came and said to me, "Come, I will show you the judgment of the great prostitute who is seated on many waters, with whom the kings of the earth have committed sexual immorality, and with the wine of whose sexual immorality the dwellers on earth have become drunk." And he carried me away in the Spirit into a wilderness, and I saw a woman sitting on a scarlet beast that was full of blasphemous names, and it had seven heads and ten horns. The woman was arrayed in purple and scarlet, and adorned with gold and jewels and pearls, holding in her hand a golden cup full of abominations and the impurities of her sexual immorality. And on her forehead was written a name of mystery: "Babylon the great, mother of prostitutes and of earth's abominations." And I saw the woman, drunk with the blood of the saints, the blood of the martyrs of Jesus. When I saw her, I marveled greatly. But the angel said to me, "Why do you marvel? I will tell you the mystery of the woman, and of the beast with seven heads and ten horns that carries her. The beast that you saw was, and is not, and is about to rise from the bottomless pit and go to destruction. And the dwellers on earth whose names have not been written in the book of life from the foundation of the world will marvel to see the beast, because it was and is not and is to come. Revelation 17:1-8 (ESV)

- He who loves wisdom makes his father glad, but a companion of prostitutes squanders his wealth. Proverbs 29:3 (ESV)
- Samson went to Gaza, and there he saw a prostitute, and he went in to her. Judges 16:1 (ESV)
- You shall not bring the fee of a prostitute or the wages of a dog into the house of the Lord your God in payment for any vow, for both of these are an abomination to the Lord your God. Deuteronomy 23:18 (ESV)
- They shall not marry a prostitute or a woman who has been defiled, neither shall they marry a woman divorced from her husband, for the priest is holy to his God. Leviticus 21:7 (ESV)
- And the Lord said to me, "Go again, love a woman who is loved by another man and is an adulteress, even as the Lord loves the children of Israel, though they turn to other gods and love cakes of raisins." So I bought her for fifteen shekels of silver and a homer and a lethech of barley. And I said to her, "You must dwell as mine for many days. You shall not play the whore, or belong to another man; so will I also be to you." For the children of Israel shall dwell many days without king or prince, without sacrifice or pillar, without ephod or household gods. Afterward the children of Israel shall return and seek the Lord their God, and David their king, and they shall come in fear to the Lord and to his goodness in the latter days. Hosea 3:1-5 (ESV)

- And all for the countless whorings of the prostitute, graceful and of deadly charms, who betrays nations with her whorings, and peoples with her charms. Nahum 3:4 (ESV)
- Rejoice not, O Israel! Exult not like the peoples; for you have played the whore, forsaking your God. You have loved a prostitute's wages on all threshing floors. Hosea 9:1 (ESV)

CPSIA information can be obtained
at www.ICGtesting.com
Printed in the USA
BVHW061020130821
614130BV00006B/15